Transitioning to Swift

Scott Gardner

Apress®

Transitioning to Swift

ISBN-13 (pbk): 978-1-4842-0407-8

ISBN-13 (electronic): 978-1-4842-0406-1

Managing Director: Welmoed Spahr
Lead Editor: Michelle Lowman
Development Editor: Douglas Pundick
Technical Reviewer: Henry Glendening

Coordinating Editor: Kevin Walter
Copy Editor: Laura Lawrie
Compositor: SPi Global
Indexer: SPi Global
Artist: SPi Global
Cover Designer: Anna Ishchenko

Distributed to the book trade worldwide by Springer Science+Business Media New York, 233 Spring Street, 6th Floor, New York, NY 10013. Phone 1-800-SPRINGER, fax (201) 348-4505, e-mail `orders-ny@springer-sbm.com`, or visit `www.springeronline.com`. Apress Media, LLC is a California LLC and the sole member (owner) is Springer Science + Business Media Finance Inc (SSBM Finance Inc). SSBM Finance Inc is a Delaware corporation.

For information on translations, please e-mail `rights@apress.com`, or visit `www.apress.com`.

Apress and friends of ED books may be purchased in bulk for academic, corporate, or promotional use. eBook versions and licenses are also available for most titles. For more information, reference our Special Bulk Sales–eBook Licensing web page at `www.apress.com/bulk-sales`.

Any source code or other supplementary material referenced by the author in this text is available to readers at `www.apress.com`. For detailed information about how to locate your book's source code, go to `www.apress.com/source-code/`.

To Lori, Charlotte, Betty, and G'Ma

Contents at a Glance

Contents

About the Author

Scott Gardner is an enterprise iOS application architect, engineer, consultant, and speaker. He is a veteran of the United States Marine Corps, and resides in the Midwest with his wife and daughter. Scott can be reached on LinkedIn: `http://linkedin.com/in/scotteg`, or on Twitter: `@scotteg`.

About the Technical Reviewer

Henry Glendening is an iOS Engineer with experience developing consumer and enterprise mobile applications. He is committed to following best practices and Apple's Human Interface Guidelines. Henry currently resides in St. Louis, MO. Follow him on Twitter at `@HAGToday`.

Acknowledgments

There are many people whom I must thank for their involvement in enabling or inspiring this book. Thank you Chris Lattner and the entire Developer Tools group, for giving us new and better ways to create amazing things. Thank you Steve Jobs, for pursuing perfection and delivering excellence.

Thank you Apress: Michelle Lowman for encouraging me to write this book; Kevin Walter for keeping us on schedule, getting things done, and tolerating my incessant changes; Douglas Pundick for sharing his masterful insight into technical writing; Laura Lawrie for ensuring grammatical correctness and breaking me of a bad habit or two along the way; Anna Ishchenko, Anne Marie Walker, Dhaneesh Kumar, Mark Powers, Matthew Moodle, and Steve Anglin, all of whom contributed to this book.

And thank you Henry Glendening for helping to ensure technical accuracy throughout the book.

Who This Book Is For

This book is for the Apple developer community—in particular, those with experience writing Objective-C code who are looking for a fast and efficient way to learn Swift by leveraging their existing skills.

Even those who have never written a line of Objective-C code can still benefit from reading, studying, and referencing this book. Objective-C code will be discussed and compared to Swift code continuously throughout the book, to help identify similarities and differences ranging from syntax nuances to entirely new approaches.

Early adoption of Swift has been strong, yet Objective-C will no doubt be around for some time. Documentation, blogs, sample code, third-party libraries, frameworks, SDKs, and open-source projects; the Apple developer community has relied on these resources for many years, and until now, they've mostly been written in Objective-C and/or C. It will take time for these resources to be migrated to Swift, and it is likely that some may never be converted. What is certain, however, is that Apple spent the last several years developing Swift to be the future of software development on their platform.

Whether your frame of reference is Objective-C or Swift, being able to recognize the similarities and differences between Objective-C and Swift code will be beneficial. One of Swift's primary goals was to break free from the chains of C. As such, it is by no means a feature parity language with Objective-C (a superset of C). In fact, Swift's design is inspired by and drawing on insights gained from several programming languages, including Ruby, Python, C#, and, of course, Objective-C. Thus, Swift is a modern programming language for modern software development. Yet having a resource to help you cross-reference code, constructs, and conventions between Objective-C and Swift will vastly broaden your capabilities. This book is that resource.

For developers with Objective-C experience, the challenge is to not only learn to write Swift, but to shift your mind-set from Objective-C to Swift. I'm reminded of the 1982 movie *Firefox*, in which Clint Eastwood must steal a Soviet fighter jet that is controlled entirely by thought, in Russian. It's not enough to be able to read and write the language. To stay competitive with the influx of new developers coming to the Apple platform *because* of Swift, one must *think* in Swift. This book will help you *grok* Swift.

Complementing the Swift Language Guide

This book is up-to-date with Swift 1.1, released on October 20, 2014. It is intended to be a practical complement to Apple's official Swift language guide: *The Swift Programming Language* (`http://bit.ly/swiftguide`). As such, comparisons, explanations, and examples will intentionally be pragmatic and actionable, aided by enough theory to help ensure a strong foundation in Swift.

Although Objective-C is a superset of C, I will refrain from covering or referencing C directly. Instead, I will refer to Objective-C, and C as used within Objective-C, collectively as Objective-C. Additionally, I will exclusively use ARC and modern Objective-C syntax.

Swift is a unique programming language, and a paradigm shift from Objective-C. Having experience with Objective-C, you will find some things comfortably familiar. However, there are many aspects of Swift that are starkly different from Objective-C, and several entirely new constructs and capabilities that did not exist or were not possible in Objective-C. It is my goal then to not just linearly map how you do something in Objective-C to how you do that same thing in Swift, but rather to improve the process of writing software by taking full advantage of Swift.

You are encouraged to type Swift code throughout this book in the playground that you will set up in Chapter 1. You are welcome to create an Xcode project or use an app such as CodeRunner (`http://bit.ly/coderunnerapp`) to run the Objective-C code. However, this is optional and will not be covered.

Let's get started. Have fun and enjoy your journey into writing powerful, expressive, and flexible code in Swift!

Chapter 1

Getting Started

In this chapter you will download, install, and set up the Apple developer tools necessary to follow along with this book. You will be introduced to the Swift programming language, by way of writing the venerable "Hello world" program and by seeing how two common actions are performed in Swift as compared with Objective-C: logging and commenting.

Installing Xcode

The minimum version of Xcode that supports writing Swift code is Xcode 6. Xcode 6 requires a Mac running OS X 10.9.3 or higher. The easiest way to install Xcode is via the App Store. From the menu select ➤ **App Store...**. Search for "xcode," which should return Xcode as the top search result. Click the **FREE** button, which will change its label to **INSTALL APP**, and click that button again to start the download and install process, as shown in Figure 1-1.

***Figure 1-1.** Drag to install Xcode in your Applications folder*

The **INSTALL APP** button label will change to **INSTALLING** while the app downloads and is installed. Weighing it at nearly 2.5 GB in size, this may take a while to download, and the only indication given within the App Store app is the button label. One way to observe the process is via the Launchpad app, which can be launched from /Applications folder if there is not a shortcut available on your Dock; Figure 1-2 demonstrates.

***Figure 1-2.** Observing the download progress via Launchpad*

Once installation is complete, a sparkle animation will appear on top of the Xcode app icon in Launchpad and the **INSTALLING** label in App Store will change to **INSTALLED**. Either click the Xcode app icon in Launchpad or locate and double-click the Xcode app icon in your /Applications folder to launch Xcode. An *Xcode and iOS SDK License Agreement* window will appear as shown in Figure 1-3. Review the terms and click **Agree** to proceed in launching Xcode.

***Figure 1-3.** Xcode and iOS SDK License Agreement*

You will be asked to enter admin credentials in order for Xcode to install necessary components to your system. After entering admin credentials, a progress window will briefly appear during that installation, and then the *Welcome to Xcode* window should appear (see Figure 1-4). If not, select from the menu **Window ➤ Welcome to Xcode**.

Creating a Playground

In the *Welcome to Xcode* window, click **Get started with a playground**, or select **File ➤ New ➤ Playground...** from the menu.

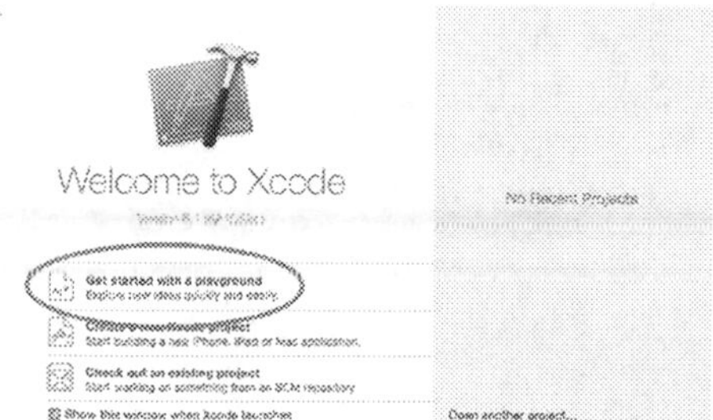

***Figure 1-4.** Welcome to Xcode*

Accept or change the suggested filename, leave the platform selection as **iOS**, and then click **Next** (Figure 1-5) and save the file to a convenient location such as your ~/Documents folder. You may find it useful to also drag this file to your Dock to create a shortcut.

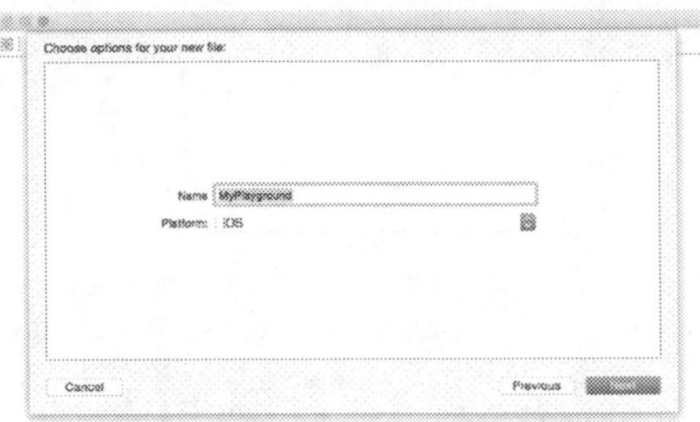

Figure 1-5. *Creating a playground*

Click **Enable** in the *Enable Developer Mode on this Mac?* window that appears, and again enter admin credentials when prompted. Your Swift playground file will appear (Figure 1-6), complete with a comment, import statement, and declaration of a string variable (more on that later).

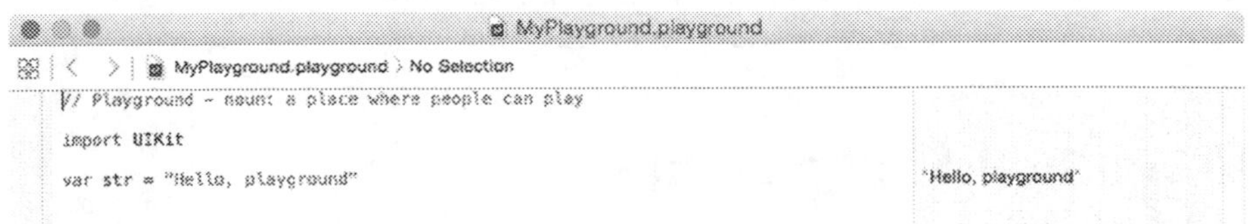

Figure 1-6. *New playground*

Notice the `import UIKit` line, but there is no `import Swift` line, as there would similarly need to be an `import Foundation` line (or some other import that imports `Foundation`) in an Objective-C source file. This is because the Swift standard library is automatically imported. You could, in fact, delete the `import UIKit` line in your playground and the existing code would still run.

Also notice the "`Hello, playground`" printout on the right, which is the results sidebar. Swift playgrounds provide an interactive environment in which you can type Swift code and immediately see the results—no Xcode project and no build and run process required. Type the following code in the line below the variable declaration:

```
println("Hello world")
```

In addition to the results sidebar, you have the option displaying console output in the Assistant Editor. I have found that displaying the Assistant Editor on the bottom makes best use of screen real estate. To specify the location of the Assistant Editor, such as on the bottom, select **View ➤ Assistant Editor ➤ Assistant Editors on Bottom**. To actually display the Assistant Editor, select **View ➤ Assistant Editor ➤ Show Assistant Editor** (Figure 1-7).

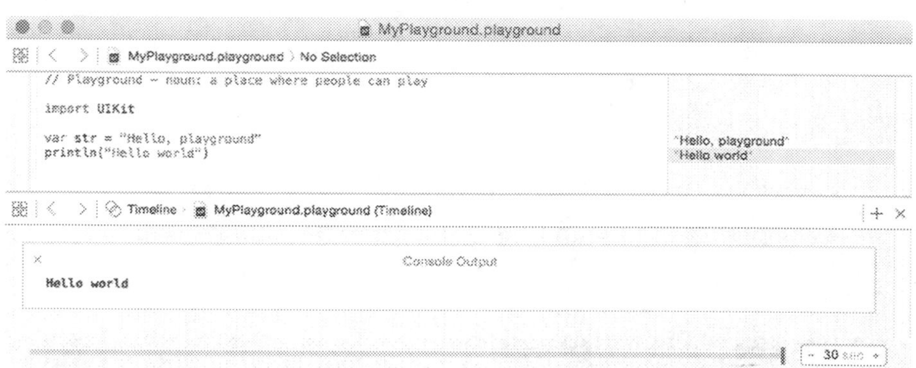

***Figure 1-7.** Playground with Assistant Editor*

Voilà! You now have a single-file, interactive Swift coding environment in which to write and observe the results of your Swift code. I've only scratched the surface of the power and versatility of Swift playgrounds, but it's all you need to know for this book. I encourage you to watch the Swift Playgrounds WWDC video at the following URL for a deeper dive into the capabilities of playgrounds:

`https://developer.apple.com/videos/wwdc/2014/?id=408`

Running a REPL

You may also set up and run a REPL — read, eval, print, loop — in order to write interactive Swift code in the command line. To enable this capability, open the Terminal app from your /Applications/Utilities folder and type `xcrun swift` (or `lldb --repl`) at the command prompt and press **return**.

You will be welcomed to the Swift REPL (Figure 1-8). Type `println("Hello world")` at the `1>` prompt and hit **return**, which will instruct the REPL to execute this function and print out, "Hello world." Type `:quit` (or even just `:q`) and press **return** to exit out of the Swift REPL and return to the command line.

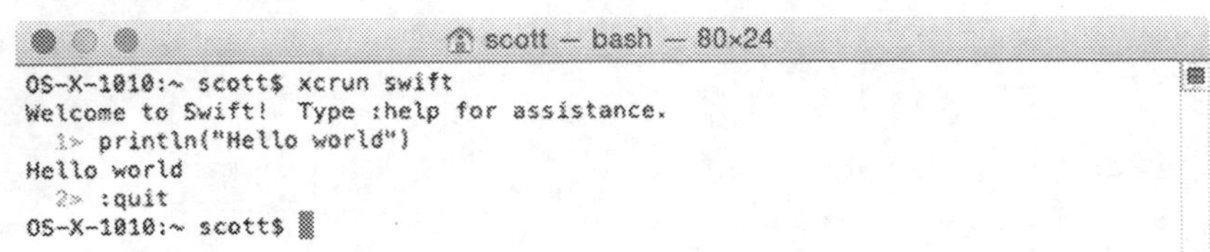

Figure 1-8. *Swift REPL*

Of course, you can also create an Xcode Swift project in the same traditional manner as you would create an Objective-C project in order to write, build, and run test/exploratory code.

Logging to the Console

Objective-C utilizes `NSLog()` to log messages to the console during runtime. `NSLog()` prefixes the provided string with a timestamp and the process ID, and adds a hard return to the end of the string. `NSLog()`'s closest counterpart in Swift is `println()` (print line). `println()` writes the provided string followed by a newline character. However, `println()` does not include a timestamp or process ID.

Swift simplifies string interpolation in `println()`. Rather than requiring you to use the correct format specifiers in the format string, followed with a comma-separated list of arguments to substitute in, you simply enclose each argument in parentheses prefixed by a backslash.

Strings and format strings in Swift are not prefixed with an @ symbol as they are in Objective-C. In the next chapter, you'll see that @ plays a far less significant role in Swift. Table 1-1 compares printing out common value types in Objective-C and Swift; syntax for creating the `helloWorld` stored value in Swift will also be covered in the next chapter.

***Table 1-1.** Printing out common value types in Objective-C and Swift*

	Objective-C	Swift
String literal	`NSLog(@"Hello world");`	`println("Hello world")`
String format	`NSString *helloWorld = @"Hello world";` `NSLog(@"%@", helloWorld);`	`let helloWorld = "Hello world"` `println("\(helloWorld)")`
Unsigned integer	`NSLog(@"numberOfObjects: %lu", (unsigned long)sectionInfo.numberOfObjects);`	`println("numberOfObjects: \(sectionInfo.numberOfObjects)")`

Swift also provides `print()` (sans the "`ln`"), which prints the supplied string without appending a newline character:

```
print("Hello ")
print("world")
// Prints "Hello world" on one line
```

> **Tip** `NSLog()` will also work in Swift if `Foundation` is imported, however, `println()` and `print()` (part of the Swift standard library) will be used throughout this book.

Similar to preprocessor macros in Objective-C, Swift includes special *literal expressions* that can be printed out to display source code and file information. Table 1-2 demonstrates; the function syntax will be covered in Chapter 6.

Table 1-2. Printing out source code and file information in Objective-C and Swift

	Objective-C	Swift

`__FILE__`	`// In MyObjCFile.m`
	`NSLog(@"%s", __FILE__);`
	`// Prints ".../MyObjCFile.m"`
		`// In MySwiftFile.swift`
		`println(__FILE__) // Prints ".../MySwiftFile.swift"`

`__LINE__`	`NSLog(@"%d", __LINE__);` `// Prints line number`	`println(__LINE__) // Prints line number`
`__COLUMN__`	N/A	`println(__COLUMN__) // Prints the column number of the first underscore of "__COLUMN__"`

`__func__`, `__FUNCTION__`	`// In SomeClass.m`
	`- (void)someMethod`
	`{`
	`NSLog(@"%s", __func__);`
	`}`
	`- (void)someOtherMethod`
	`{`
	`[self someMethod]; // Prints "-[SomeClass someMethod]"`
	`}`
		`func someFunction() {`
		`println(__FUNCTION__)`
		`}`
		`someFunction() // Prints "someFunction()"`

Adding Comments

The syntax for writing single and multiline comments in Objective-C and Swift is identical. Although Objective-C and Swift both allow nesting single-line comments within multiline comments, Swift adds the ability to nest multiline comments within multiline comments.

Swift does not include a preprocessor as does Objective-C, so preprocessor directives such as `#pragma marks` are not available. In place of `#pragma marks`, Xcode 6+ supports `// MARK:`, `//MARK: -`, `// TODO:`, and `// FIXME:` landmarks in Swift source files to help organize code and provide visual separation in the jump bar. Although these landmarks are also recognized in Objective-C source files, in Swift source files, Xcode will also create a line separator for `// MARK:` and a line separate preceeding any text typed after the dash for `// MARK: -`, thereby making them suitable replacements for `#pragma marks`. Table 1-3 compares these commenting capabilities in Objective-C and Swift, followed by screenshots of the resulting Xcode jump bars for Objective-C and Swift source files in Figures 1-9 and 1-10.

Table 1-3. Entering comments in Objective-C and Swift

Objective-C	Swift
// Single line comment	// Single line comment
/* This is a multiline comment */	/* This is a multiline comment */
/* This is a multiline... // SINGLE LINE COMMENT ...comment */	/* This is a multiline... // SINGLE LINE COMMENT ...comment */
N/A	/* This is a multiline... /* ANOTHER MULTILINE COMMENT */ ...comment */

#pragma // Creates a line separator in the jump bar
#pragma mark - This is a mark preceeded by a separator
// TODO: Do this
// FIXME: Fix this
	// MARK: This is a mark
	// MARK: - This is a mark preceeded by a separator
	// TODO: Do this
	// FIXME: Fix this

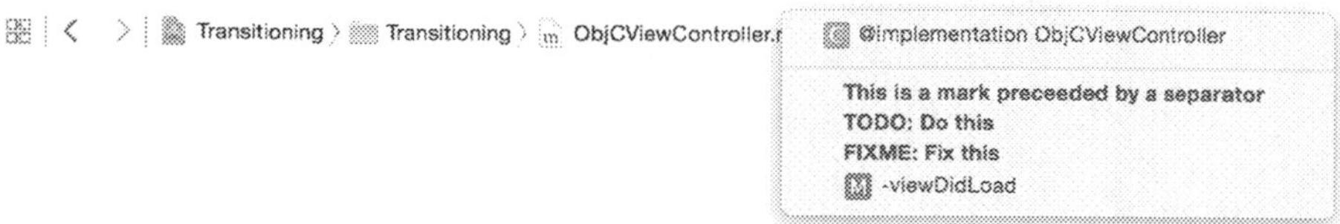

Figure 1-9. *Jump bar in Xcode 6 for an Objective-C source file*

Figure 1-10. *Jump bar in Xcode 6 for a Swift source file*

Xcode 6 also recognizes comments beginning with either `/**` or `///`, placed atop a line or block of code, as documentation comments. For proper formatting, enter the description on a new line followed by a blank line. Document parameters with `:param:` and return values with `:returns:`. Additionally, sections can be added to the description using `:sectionTitle:`, and bullets can be added using `- :bulletTitle:` (`* :bulletTitle:` also works), replacing `sectionTitle` and `bulletTitle` with whatever titles you want. See Figure 1-11 (disregard the function syntax for now).

```
/**
Converts an integer to a string

:section 1: section content...
:section 2: section content...
- :bullet 1: bullet content...
:param: input an integer
:returns: a string
*/
func myFunc(input: Int) -> String {
    let stringValue = "\(input)"
    return stringValue
}
```

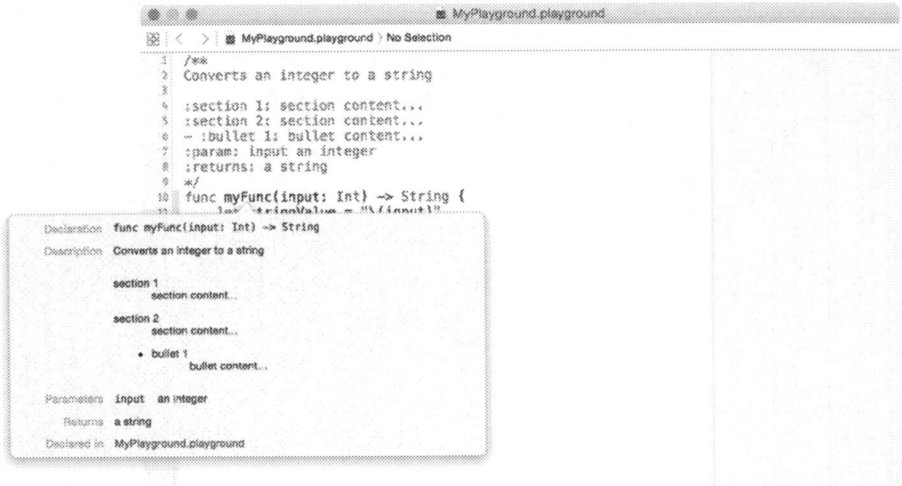

***Figure 1-11.** Document comment in a Swift source file*

Although I'll leave it as an exercise for those interested to further explore, I'd be remiss not to at least mention an excellent Xcode plugin that simplifies this process, VVDocumenter-Xcode (`https://github.com/onevcat/VVDocumenter-Xcode`), which can be conveniently installed via Alcatraz (`http://alcatraz.io`).

Using Dot Notation

There remains a healthy debate among Objective-C developers regarding the use of dot versus bracket notation for accessing properties (getters and setters). Prior to iOS 8, certain methods—such as `count` for `NSArray`, `NSDictionary`, and others—would compile even if called using dot notation (e.g., `myArray.count`). This was regarded by some (myself included) as being syntactically incorrect. However, with iOS 8, most if not all of these methods have been converted to properties, thus eschewing the controversy. That said, Swift exclusively uses dot syntax to access properties and members, and to call methods.

Summary

In this chapter you installed the Apple developer tools necessary to write Swift code and you created a playground and REPL to enable writing *interactive* Swift code. You also learned how to perform two very common actions in Swift: logging and commenting. You are now equipped to start programming in Swift, beginning in the next chapter with declaring variables and constants to store values.

Chapter 2

Declaring Variables and Constants

Programming is largely about solving problems with math, and to do that you need to store values and represent them in your algorithms. Most programming languages share a similar approach to storing values, yet the simplicity or terseness of syntax seems to be a differentiator amongst modern languages. Swift delivers a concise yet logical syntax that creates a harmonious balance between the coder and the compiler. This chapter will show you how to create stored values in Swift as compared with Objective-C, beginning with an explanation of how the two languages differ in approach.

> **Note** The phrase "stored value" is used interchangeably with "variable" and/or "constant" throughout this book.

Value Types and Reference Types

Objective-C, being a superset of C, deals in scalar values (such as `int`, `float`, and `char`), `typedef` wrappers around scalar values (for example, `NSInteger` and `CGFloat`), object pointer references (seminally, `NSObject`), and even object pointer reference wrappers around scalar values (`NSNumber`). This is an oversimplification, but the point to be taken here is that storing values in Objective-C can be handled in a variety of different ways. Swift, by contrast, consists of two fundamental categories: value types and reference types.

Value types include structures and enumerations. All of Swift's basic data types—integers, floating-point numbers, booleans, strings, arrays, and dictionaries—are implemented as structures. Characters are implemented as enumerations. Classes and closures are reference types. Figure 2-1 provides a breakdown of value types and reference types in Swift. Of the types listed in the figure, you may not be familiar with tuples or closures, which will be covered in the next chapter and in Chapter 5, respectively.

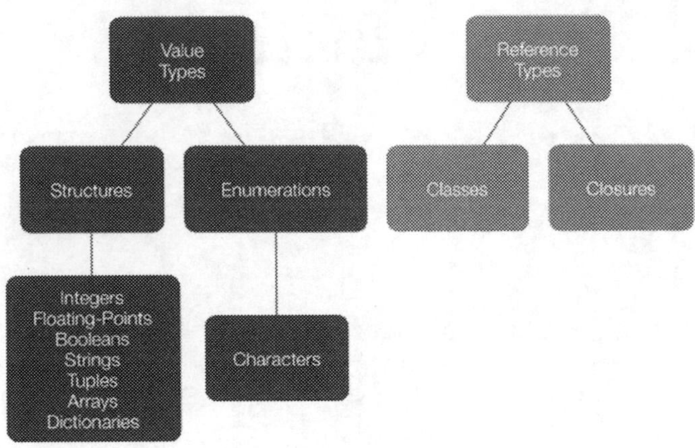

***Figure 2-1.** Value types and reference types in Swift*

A value type is copied, such as when assigned to a variable or when passed to a method. Behind the scenes, Swift will actually only perform a copy when it is absolutely necessary to do so. But for all intents and purposes, consider that you are always passing value types by copy. Coming from Objective-C, you may be used to using the `copy` attribute when creating immutable properties of classes such as `NSString` that have mutable counterparts, to ensure that your property maintains its own state. This is automatic in Swift with all value types including `String`, for example.

Conversely, a reference type is always passed around by reference to the same instance. A reference type passed in to a method, for example, is the same instance referred to within the method as external to it.

Named Types and Compound Types

Swift also classifies types as being either named or compound. Named types can, well, be named when they are defined. Named types can also have methods associated with them and be extended; see Chapters 7, 8, and 9 for details. Classes, structures, enumerations, and protocols are named types. Compound types are not named, as they are defined in the Swift language itself. Function types and tuples are compound types. Function types represent closures, functions (also known as named closures), and methods (functions within a class); see Chapter 6 for details. Tuple types are comma-separated lists enclosed in parentheses.

Being aware of this lexical grouping may be of less practical importance than knowing whether an item you're dealing with is passed around in your code as a copy or as a reference to the same instance. Just remember that only class types are passed by reference; everything else is passed by copy. Figure 2-2 provides a breakdown of named types and compound types in Swift.

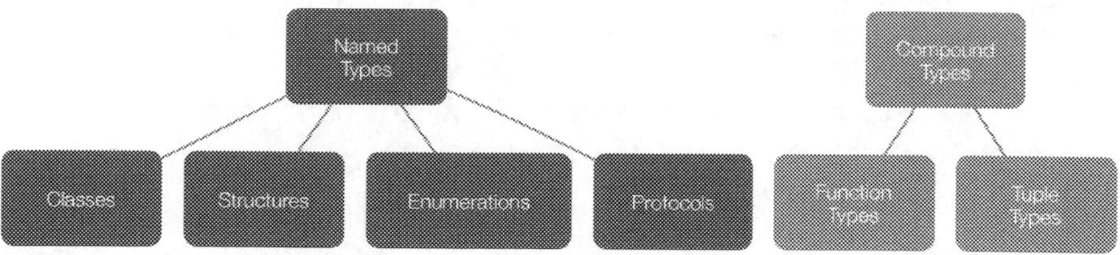

***Figure 2-2.** Named types and compound types in Swift*

Naming

Nearly any character can be used to name a named type, including most Unicode characters but excluding mathematical symbols, arrows, and line- and box- or other invalid Unicode characters. Like Objective-C, Swift names cannot begin with a number, although they can be included elsewhere within the name. You can even use reserved words as names in Swift, simply by enclosing the name in back ticks (`); however, this is generally discouraged. Carrying forward tradition, variable and constant names should begin with a lower case letter and use camel case notation.

Mutability

Objective-C offers several classes in both "regular" and mutable versions, such as NSString/NSMutableString, NSArray/NSMutableArray, and so on. In Swift, mutability is determined when you create an instance, not by choice of class. An instance is declared as being either a variable or constant, thus establishing whether it can or cannot be changed.

Variables are declared using the var keyword and are mutable. Constants are immutable and declared using the let keyword. Constants must be assigned a value when declared, with one exception: when declaring properties, a constant property can be declared without assigning a value. This is because it is init()'s job to ensure that all properties are assigned a value; see Chapter 7 for details.

Although it is possible to apply the const keyword from C to a variable in Objective-C to make it immutable, in practice this is most commonly done at the global level within a class, for example, to create string constants that will take advantage of code completion versus using literal strings which are prone to typo-based errors. In Swift, constants are used ubiquitously. Apple advises to always declare a stored value as a constant when you know its value is not going to change, because doing so aids performance and also better conveys the intended use of a stored value.

Table 2-1 shows how to create a variable and constant in Swift.

***Table 2-1.** Creating variable and constant stored values in Swift*

Variable	`var valueThatMayChange = "Hello "`
Constant	`let valueThatWillNotChange = "Hello world"`

Declaring Type

To specifically declare the type of a stored value, follow the name with a colon and then the type annotation—for example, to create a variable named "greeting" that explicitly is of type String:

```
var greeting: String = "Hello world"
```

Unlike Objective-C, which requires the type to be explicitly declared when creating an instance, Swift can infer the type from the value assigned to the instance. You can specifically declare the type if you want to—you just don't have to, as long as it can be inferred by the value being assigned. This helps to make Swift a type safe language. The previous greeting variable could have been created as implicitly of type `String` like this:

```
var greeting = "Hello world"
```

An exception to this rule is with the `Character` type. A `Character` value will be inferred to be of type `String` unless explicitly typed `Character`:

```
let eAcute1 = "é"
println(_stdlib_getDemangledTypeName(eAcute1)) // Prints "Swift.String"
let eAcute2: Character = "é"
println(_stdlib_getDemangledTypeName(eAcute2)) // Prints "Swift.Character"
```

> **Tip** In Xcode, you can **option** + **click** on a stored value to display its type in a popup.

Similar to `id` in Objective-C, you can declare a variable or constant in Swift as type `AnyObject` to indicate that it can be an instance of any class type. Furthermore, in Swift you can declare a variable or constant as type `Any` to indicate that it can be of any type except a function type. Apple discourages this in favor of the code clarity achieved by being explicit about types. And in the case of constants, one plausible usage is for constant stored properties, which can be declared with assignment deferred to `init()`; see Chapter 7 for details.

Multiple stored values can be declared in a comma-separated list on one line. Values not explicitly declared as of a type are inferred to be of the first type specified:

```
var red, green, blue, alpha: Double // All values are of type Double
var firstName, lastName: String, birthYear, birthMonth, birthDay: Int
// firstName and lastName are of type String; birthYear, birthMonth, and
birthDay are of type Int
```

Defining Type

In Objective-C, a `typedef` statement can be used to define a new data type—or redefine an existing type—as another existing type. Although this is used mostly with enumerations, structures, and blocks, a `typedef` can be used to define any type. Swift similarly uses `typealias` to define an alternative name for any existing type, although note use of the assignment operator (=). Table 2-2 compares defining types in Objective-C and Swift.

Table 2-2 also demonstrates that structures in Swift can have properties; even the types themselves can have properties. In this case, UInt has a min type property (see Chapter 7 for details).

***Table 2-2.** Defining types in Objective-C and Swift*

Objective-C	`typedef NSInteger VolumeLevel;` `VolumeLevel volume = 0;`
Swift	`typealias VolumeLevel = UInt` `let volume = VolumeLevel.min`

Tip In Xcode, you can **command** + **click** on a target such as UInt to transfer to its definition. Doing so reveals that UInt is implemented as a struct of type UnsignedIntegerType. And even though you may not be familiar with all the syntax yet, it is fairly easy to discern that UInt has both max and min entries (i.e., type properties):

```
struct UInt : UnsignedIntegerType {
  // ...
  static var max: UInt { get }
  static var min: UInt { get }
}
```

Declaration Attributes

Swift includes several attributes that can be used to provide additional information about a stored value being declared, which will be displayed in a popup when **option** + **click**ing on the stored value, or in an error message if applicable. While these attributes can be used with independent stored values (e.g., declared in a global scope), they are more likely to be used and encountered with properties of classes, structures, and enumerations; see Chapter 7 for additional information about these types and declaration attribute usage examples. One attribute in particular, @availability, takes two or more arguments to specify the applicable platform(s), followed by one or more additional arguments in comma-separated list. The first argument of the @availability attribute indicates the applicable platform, e.g., iOS, iOSApplicationExtension, or OSX; alternatively, an asterisk (*) can be used to indicate that the @availability attribute is applicable to all platforms. The remaining arguments will include a value assignment. Table 2-3 provides examples of using the @availability declaration attribute in stored value declarations.

Table 2-3. Examples of using the `@availability` declaration attribute with stored value declarations in Swift

Introduced	`@availability(iOS, introduced=1.0) var anIOSOnlyValue: Int`
Deprecated with message	`@availability(OSX, deprecated=1.0, message="anUnusedOSXOnlyTuple has been deprecated and will be removed in a future release. Use aUsefulOSXOnlyTuple(Double, String) instead.") var anUnusedOSXOnlyTuple: (Int, String)`
Obsoleted	`@availability(*, obsoleted=1.0) var anUnavailableValue: String` `anUnavailableValue = "Hello" // error: 'anUnavailableValue' is unavailable`

The `renamed` `@availability` argument can be used in conjunction with a `typealias` to indicate a custom type (such as a custom class, structure, or enumeration type) has been renamed, along with an alias to the old name so that existing code continues to work; an example will be provided in Chapter 7. `@NSCopying` and `@noreturn` attributes are also available for use with properties and functions, respectively. Chapter 6 will cover `@noreturn` and Chapter 7 will cover `@NSCopying`. The `@objc` declaration attribute can be used to mark an entity as being available to Objective-C source code within the same module—which is required for protocols containing optional requirements; Chapters 7 and 8 will examine these use cases.

Additional declaration attributes are available for use in Xcode projects, of which coverage is beyond the scope of this book, including `@UIApplicationMain`, `@NSManaged`, `@IBAction`, `@IBInspectable`, `@IBAction`, and `@IBDesignable`. *Beginning iPhone Development with Swift* (`http://www.apress.com/9781484204108`) provides coverage of `@UIAppliationMain` and `@IBAction`, and here are some shortlinks to additional helpful resources:

```
http://bit.ly/whatsNewInInterfaceBuilder
http://bit.ly/whatsNewInInterfaceBuilderTextVersion
http://bit.ly/NSManagedObjectAttribute
```

@, *, and ;

The `@` symbol is used ubiquitously in Objective-C, as an object string format specifier (e.g., for use in `-[NSString stringWithFormat:]`), and to create data types such as `NSString`, `NSNumber`, `NSArray`, and `NSDictionary` using Objective-C literal syntax. Such is not the case in Swift, where `@` is used only as a prefix for certain declaration attributes, as mentioned in the previous section, Declaration Attribute.

Asterisks are all but gone, save for their continued use in operators, multiline comments, and declaration attributes. Swift abstracts pointer management for reference types such that a variable or constant that refers to an instance of a reference type is not a direct pointer to an address in memory as in Objective-C, and you do not write an asterisk to indicate that a variable or constant is a reference type.

Semicolons are no longer required at the end of statements, except when including multiple statements on the same line, such as in a `for` loop. You can still end your statements with semicolons if you wish; however, this "syntactic noise" is discouraged.

Declaring Values

Number values in Swift can optionally use underscores to increase readability of long numbers.

Apple encourages using `Int` instead of `UInt`, even if a stored integer value is intended to be non-negative, unless you specifically require an unsigned integer type or an integer type of a specific size (`Int` can store any value between -2,147,483,648 and 2,147,483,647); this aids in code consistency and interoperability.

Swift's `Double` represents a 64-bit floating-point number with at least 15 decimal points precision, versus `Float`, which represents a 32-bit floating-point number of as little as 6 decimal digits precision. Swift will infer a floating-point number as type `Double` unless explicitly declared as type `Float`:

```
let pi = 3.14159 // pi is inferred to be of type Double
let pi: Float = 3.14159 // pi is explicity declared as a Float
```

Whereas booleans in Objective-C are assigned the value `YES` or `NO`, Swift assigns `true` or `false`.

Tables 2-4 and 2-5 compare creating variables and constants in Objective-C and Swift. Recognizing that creating constants in Objective-C is far less common than in Swift, the intention is to show as close a match syntactically as possible between the two languages.

Table 2-4. Creating mutable variables in Objective-C and Swift

	Objective-C	Swift
Signed integer	`NSInteger x = -1;` `NSNumber *x = @-1;`	`var x = -1`
Unsigned integer	`NSUInteger x = 1000000;` `NSNumber *x = @1000000;`	`var x: UInt = 1_000_000`
Floating-point	`CGFloat pi = 3.14159f;` `NSNumber *pi = @3.144159f;`	`var π = 3.14159`
Boolean	`BOOL success = YES;` `NSNumber *success = @YES;`	`var 👍 = true`
Character	`char a = 'a';` `NSNumber *a = @'a';`	`var a: Character = "ⓐ"`
String	`NSMutableString *greeting =` `[@"Hello" mutableCopy];`	`var greeting = "Hello"`
id	`id greeting = @"Hello world";`	`var greeting: AnyObject` `= "Hello 🌎"`

Table 2-5. Creating immutable constants in Objective-C and Swift

	Objective-C	Swift
Signed integer	`const NSInteger x = -1;` `const NSNumber *x = @-1;`	`let x: = -1`
Unsigned integer	`const NSUInteger x = 1000000;` `const NSNumber *x = @1000000;`	`let x: UInt = 1_000_000`
Floating-point	`const CGFloat x = 5.0f;` `const NSNumber *x = @1.0f;`	`let p = 3.14159`
Boolean	`const BOOL success = YES;` `const NSNumber *success = @YES;`	`let 👍 = true`
Character	`const char a = 'a';` `const NSNumber *a = @'a';`	`let a: Character = "ⓐ"`
String	`NSString *greeting = @"Hello";`	`let greeting = "Hello"`
id	`const id greeting = @"Hello` `world";`	`let greeting: AnyObject` `= "Hello 🌎"`

> **Tip** A handy keyboard shortcut to know is **command** + **control** + **spacebar** to pull up the special characters menu. Continuing a keyboard-driven approach, you can then just type what you're looking for (e.g., "thumb" or "earth"), use the arrow keys to navigate, and press **return** to insert the selected character.

It's worth noting that Swift's `Character` type is actually a sequence of one or more Unicode scalars—also known as an *extended grapheme cluster*—that (singularly or combined) represent a single character. And a Swift `String` type is simply a sequence of those clusters. You can create characters by typing in the actual Unicode character (as seen in the previous tables), or you can use the string interpolation syntax: `\u{N}`, where `N` is the hexadecimal portion of the Unicode scalar value, wherein it is also ok to omit leading 0s. For example, to represent the letter "a" (Unicode scalar U+0061), use `\u{61}`. Additionally, a character with an accent, such as "é," can be represented by a single Unicode scalar or a pair of scalars separately representing the "e" and the accent. And, although these two representations of "é" are made up of different clusters, they are canonically equivalent—that is, they have the same linguistic meaning—and, therefore, Swift considers them equal:

```
let eAcute1 = "\u{E9}"
let eAcute2 = "\u{65}\u{301}"
println(eAcute1 == eAcute2) // Prints "true"

let string1 = "The e acute character is \u{E9}"
let string2: String = "The e acute character is \u{65}\u{301}"
println(string1 == string2) // Prints "true"
```

Writing Numeric Literals

Numeric literals include floating-point and integer literals with optional exponents, binary integer literals, and hexadecimal numeric (integer or floating-point) literals with optional exponents. All of these are written the same way in Swift as they are in Objective-C. However, octal integer literals are written with the `0o` (zero and letter "o") prefix in Swift versus a `0` alone in Objective-C. Table 2-5 provides examples of writing numeric literals in Objective-C and Swift.

Table 2-6. Writing numeric literals in Objective-C and Swift

	Objective-C	Swift

Floating-point, integer	`CGFloat oneTwentyDouble = 1.2e2; // 120.0`
	`NSInteger oneTwentyInt = 1.2e2; // 120`
	`CGFloat negativeOneTwenty = -1.2e2; // -120.0`
		`let oneTwentyDouble = 1.2e2 // 120.0`
		`let oneTwentyInt: Int = 1.2e2 // 120`
		`let negativeOneTwenty = -1.2e2 // -120.0`

Binary	`NSInteger binary15 = 0b1111; // 15` `NSInteger negativeBinary15 = -0b1111; // -15`	`let binary15 = 0b1111 // 15` `let negativeBinary15 = -0b1111 // -15`
Octal	`NSInteger octal15 = 017; // 15` `NSInteger negativeOctal15 = -017; // -15`	`let octal15 = 0o17 // 15` `let negativeOctal15 = -0o17 // -15`

Hexadecimal	`NSInteger hex15 = 0xf; // 15`
	`NSInteger negativeHex15 = -0xf; // -15`
	`CGFloat hexSixty = 0xfp2; // 60`
	`CGFloat hexThreePointSevenFive = 0xfp-2; // 3.75`
	`CGFloat hexFifteenPointFive = 0xf.8p0;`
		`let hex15 = 0xf // 15`
		`let negativeHex15 = -0xf // -15`
		`let hexSixty = 0xfp2 // 60`
		`let hexThreePointSevenFive = 0xfp-2 // 3.75`
		`let hexFifteenPointFive = 0xf.8p0`

Access Control

Although Objective-C has long offered compile-time instance variable access control, properties and methods have lacked this feature. In recent years, Apple has also boosted encouragement of using properties instead of instance variables. As a result, access control in Objective-C has seen minimal usage as compared with other languages. Still, Objective-C's instance variable access control directives adhere to traditional usage patterns: `@public`, which Apple warns should never be used as it violates the principle of encapsulation, `@protected` (the default) that limits access to class in which the instance variable is declared and its subclasses, and `@private`, which limits access to the declaring class alone.

Swift, by contrast, offers comprehensive access control, taking a somewhat avante-garde approach. Because access control is often something of an advanced interest—such as for framework and library development—and because the nature of Swift's implementation of access control is generally more complex, with various exceptions for things like default access levels, an entire chapter (Chapter 10) is dedicated to its coverage.

Protocol Adoption

A basic introduction to declaring protocol adoption is provided here. Complete coverage of protocols can be found in Chapter 8.

In Objective-C, to create a variable or constant and declare that it adopts one or more protocols, you would create the variable or constant as type `id` and enclose one or more protocols in a comma-separated list within angle brackets.

In Swift, you can declare that a variable or constant adopts a protocol in the same manner as declaring type. This is not generally necessary thanks to Swift's type inference, although you do need to cast the assigned value using the `as` operator. Table 2-7 compares creating a stored value that is of a type that adopts a protocol in Objective-C and Swift.

Table 2-7. Creating a stored value with protocol adoption in Objective-C and Swift

Objective-C	`id <NSFetchedResultsSectionInfo> sectionInfo = [self.fetchedResultsController.sections[section];`
Swift	`let sectionInfo = self.fetchedResultsController. sections[section] as NSFetchedResultsSectionInfo`

`nil` and Optionals

All this time you have been assigning a value during declaration of a variable or constant. Although constants must be assigned a value when declared (except properties, as previously noted), variables do not require value assignment during declaration. How you go about doing this in Swift is different than in Objective-C, however. In Objective-C, a variable declared without assigning a value is `nil` (actually a pointer to `nil`). In Swift, `nil` literally means no value.

In order for a variable (of any type) to optionally be able to store a value or be `nil`, its type must be marked as an optional. This is done by explicitly declaring the type followed with a ? (no space):

```
var anEmptyStringForNow: String?
```

This is a syntactic shortcut for declaring the variable of type `Optional` followed by angle brackets enclosing the value type:

```
var anEmptyStringForNow: Optional<String>
```

The former question mark syntax is preferred for declaring an optional. There will be plenty of opportunity to use the latter syntax while taking advantage of Swift's generic programming capabilities to create functions and types that are more flexible and reusable than in Objective-C; see chapters Chapter 11 for details.

A variable declared as optional without assigning a value is `nil`. It can subsequently be assigned a value of its specified type or be set to `nil` again. A constant can also be declared as optional, although because a constant is immutable, this is of lesser practical value:

```
var myConditionalInt: Int?
myConditionalInt = 1
myConditionalInt = nil
```

An optional must be *unwrapped* in order to access its value, and this can be done explicitly, implicitly, via optional binding, or during optional chaining. To explicitly unwrap an optional, suffix it with an `!`, also referred to as "forced unwrapping":

```
var myInt1: Int? = 1
var myInt2: Int? = 2
let sum = myInt1! + myInt2!
```

Operators such as + will be covered in Chapter 4.

If you are certain that an optional will always have a value, you can implicitly unwrap the optional during declaration by suffixing the type with an `!`, and this avoids having to force unwrap the optional to access its value every time:

```
var myInt1: Int!
myInt1 = 1
let myInt2: Int! = 2
let sum = myInt1 + myInt2
```

There are some useful syntax shortcuts for using optionals in controlling program flow that will be covered in Chapter 5.

Syntax Reference

Figure 2-3 summarizes the syntax for creating variables and constants in Swift. Italicized text indicates optional components.

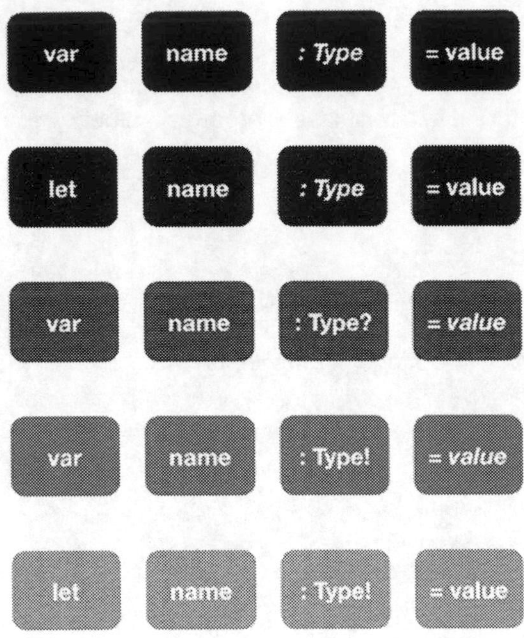

***Figure 2-3.** Syntax for creating variables and constants in Swift*

Summary

This chapter provided an overview of Swift value types and explained how to create variables and constants in Swift. Swift is designed to be a modern programming language that blends simplified syntax, powerful capabilities, and strong compiler support, to help you write more succinct and readable code that is also less prone to runtime errors. After reading this chapter and writing the example code in your Swift playground or REPL, you should be comfortable with how to declare, store, and print out values in Swift. The side-by-side nature used to compare Objective-C and Swift code in this chapter will be used throughout the book.

Chapter 3

Working with Strings and Collections

Chapter 2 introduced the basic structure of Swift and explained the different types, mutability versus immutability, and notable syntax changes, among other things. This chapter builds on that foundation of knowledge, focusing on creating and manipulating strings and collections of values.

Working with Strings

The Swift `String` value type is bridged seamlessly to Objective-C's `NSString` class, meaning that any `NSString` method can be called on a `String` value, and a `String` value can be used with any API that expects an `NSString` instance. However, this does not mean that there is complete interchangability between `String` and `NSString`. For example, `String` methods such as `toInt()()`, computed properties such as `endIndex`, and global functions such as `countElements()` will not work with an `NSString` instance.

Following an examination of the salient differences between Swift's `String` type and Objective-C's `NSString` and `NSMutableString` classes, Table 3-1 provides several examples that compare `NSString` and `NSMutableString` methods and techniques with Swift `String` equivalents (see Chapter 5 for additional coverage of the conditional syntax used in some of the examples).

Much as in Objective-C, strings in Swift can be created in a variety of ways, including as empty strings, literal strings, and using format strings. Remember that the mutability of a `String` value in Swift is determined by whether it is initialized as a variable (`var`) or constant (`let`), versus by class selection in Objective-C (`NSMutableString` and `NSString`).

As in Objective-C and mentioned in the last chapter, a String type in Swift is actually an ordered collection (i.e., sequence) of Unicode characters (specifically, Character values in Swift). Exploring String's definition (such as by **command** + **click**ing on a String type declaration in Xcode) reveals that String is actually a simple struct type accompanied by a series of extensions:

```
struct String {
  init()
}

extension String : CollectionType {
// ...
```

Clicking into CollectionType's definition shows that it is a protocol, and so this extension adopts and conforms to the CollectionType protocol, which (clicking through to its definition) conforms to the _CollectionType protocol, which is the input type expected by the global countElements() function. Therefore, countElements() can be called, passing a String type, and it will return the count of Character values that make up the string:

```
let abcString = "ABC"
countElements(abcString) // 3
```

> **Note** A protocol in Swift is—much as in Objective-C—simply a contract. By adopting a protocol in Swift, a type is agreeing to implement the protocol's requirements. Chapter 8 will cover protocols in full.

countElements() should normally suffice when the need to get a String value's length arises. Remember from the last chapter, however, that the Character type represents a sequence of *extended grapheme clusters* that are combined to produce a single human-readable character. countElements() counts Character values, not the individual clusters, which could be one or more per each Character value. Reading further into the extension that adopts the CollectionType protocol will disclose how, then, to get the length of a String value in terms of the count of individual clusters:

```
extension String : CollectionType {
  struct Index : BidirectionalIndexType, Comparable, Reflectable {
    func successor() -> String.Index
    func predecessor() -> String.Index
    func getMirror() -> MirrorType
  }
```

```
  var startIndex: String.Index { get }
  var endIndex: String.Index { get }
  subscript (i: String.Index) -> Character { get }
  func generate() -> IndexingGenerator<String>
}
```

Even though much of this syntax may be new to you at this point, the lines defining the vars `startIndex` and `endIndex` should look familiar. These are *computed properties* that return the position of the index *before* the first cluster, and position of the index *after* the last cluster, respectively (computed properties will be further covered in Chapter 7):

```
let abcString = "ABC"
abcString.startIndex // 0
abcString.endIndex   // 3
```

Notice that, because `endIndex` is the position of the index after the last character, it also happens to be equal to the length of the string. This is not always the case, however:

```
let circledStar: Character = "\u{2606}\u{20DD}" // ☆⃝
```

`circledStar` is a single `Character` value made up of two clusters: a white star (U+2606) and a combining enclosing circle (U+20DD). Let's create a `String` from `circledStar` and compare the results of `countElements()` and `endIndex`:

```
let circledStarString = "\(circledStar)"
countElements(circledStarString) // 1
circledStarString.endIndex // 2
```

All that said, Swift's exact counterpart to Objective-C's `NSString length` property is `String`'s `utf16Count` computed property, because both are based on the number of 16-bit code units, not the number of Unicode extended grapheme clusters. It is therefore possible that two `String` values made up using different clusters are considered equal and `countElements()` returns the same result; however, their `endIndex` and `utf16Count` properties will be different. In the following example, the character "é" is created using a single cluster (U+00E9) in `string1`, and two clusters (U+0065 for "e" and U+0301 for the combining acute accent) in `string2`:

```
let string1 = "The e acute character is \u{E9}" // "é"
let string2 = "The e acute character is \u{65}\u{301}" // "é"
println(countElements(string1) == countElements(string2)) // Prints "true"
println(string1.endIndex == string2.endIndex) // Prints "false"
println(string1.endIndex) // Prints "26"
```

```
println(string2.endIndex) // Prints "27"
println(string1.utf16Count == string2.utf16Count) // Prints "false"
println(string1.utf16Count) // Prints "26"
println(string2.utf16Count) // Prints "27"
```

The Swift `String` type also has an `isEmpty` computed property, which can be used to determine if a string is, well, empty. Similar to Objective-C's `-[NSString hasPrefix]` and `-[NSString hasSuffix]` methods, Swift `String` types also have `hasPrefix()` and `hasSuffix()` methods.

`String` has several `init()` methods that can be used to create strings from integer value types, as well as a variety of `init()` methods that use format strings (wherein the format string arguments can either be provided as a comma-separated list or in an array). `String` also has a `toInt()` method that will attempt to convert a `String` value to an `Int` value. Because this attempt may fail, an optional `Int?` is returned. Remember to unwrap the optional before use. Swift does not currently offer a `toDouble()` method; however, an example of how to convert a String value to a `Double` value (by casting to an `NSString` and using `NSString` API) is provided in Table 3-1.

Swift strings can be concatenated using the + and += operators. A `Character` value can be appended to a String value using the `append()` method.

> **Note** A character literal assigned to a variable or constant will be implicitly inferred to be of type `String`. Explicitly cast a character as type `Character` as necessary.

Remember that `NSString` instances in Objective-C are passed by reference unless explicitly copied, whereas `String` values in Swift are always passed by copy.

> **Tip** Press **option** + **p** to type the character "π."

Table 3-1. *Comparing Objective-C* `NSString` *and* `NSMutableString` *methods and techniques to Swift* `String` *equivalents*

	Objective-C	Swift

Create	`NSString *string1 = @"Hello world!";`
	`NSMutableString *string2 = [NSMutableString new];`
	`NSMutableString *string3 = [@"" mutableCopy];`
		`let string1 = "Hello world!"`
		`var string2 = String()`
		`var string3 = ""`

Introspect and interpolate	`NSLog(@"%lu", (unsigned long) string1.length); // Prints "12"`
	`NSLog(@"%i", !string2. length); // Prints "1"`
	`NSLog(@"%i", [string1 hasPrefix:@"Hello"]);`
	`// Prints "1"`
	`NSLog(@"%i", [string1 hasSuffix:@"earth!"]);`
	`// Prints "0"`
	`CGFloat C = 9.42f;`
	`NSInteger d = 3;`
	`NSLog(@"π is equal to %.2f", C / d); // Prints "π is equal to 3.14"`
	`NSLog(@"π is equal to %.2f", 3.14159265358979323846);`
	`// Prints "π is equal to 3.14"`
		`import Foundation`
		`println(string1.utf16Count)`
		`// Prints "12"`
		`println(countElements(string1))`
		`// Prints "12"`
		`println(string2.isEmpty)`
		`// Prints "true"`
		`println(string1. hasPrefix("Hello")) // Prints true`
		`println(string1. hasSuffix("earth!")) // Prints false`
		`let C = 9.42`
		`let d = 3.0`
		`println("π is equal to \(C / d)")`
		`// Prints "π is equal to 3.14"`
		`let π = String(format: "%.2f", 3.14159265358979323846)`
		`println("π is equal to \(π)")`
		`// Prints "π is equal to 3.14"`

Compare	`if ([string2 isEqualToString:string3]) {`
	`NSLog(@"string2 equals string3");`
	`}`
	`// Prints "string2 equals string3"`
		`if string2 == string3 {`
		`println("string2 equals string3")`
		`}`
		`// Prints "string2 equals string3"`

Convert	`NSString *fiveString = [@5 stringValue]; // "5"`
	`NSInteger five = [fiveString integerValue];`
		`let fiveString = "\(5)" // "5"`
		`let five = fiveString.toInt()!`
		`let pi = Double((π as NSString). doubleValue) // 3.14`

(*continued*)

Table 3-1. (*continued*)

	Objective-C	Swift

Copy and mutate	`NSMutableString *string4 = [string1 mutableCopy];`
	`[string4 appendFormat:@" Am I alone?"];`
	`NSLog(@"%@", string1);`
	`// Prints "Hello world!"`
	`NSLog(@"%@", string4);`
	`// Prints "Hello world! Am I alone?"`
	`NSMutableString *string5 = string4;`
	`[string5 replaceCharactersInRange:NSMakeRange(13, 10) withString:@"How do you like me now"];`
	`if ([string4 isEqualToString:string5]) {`
	`NSLog(@"%@", string5);`
	`}`
	`// Prints "Hello world! How do you like me now?"`
		`var string4 = string1`
		`string4 += " Am I alone?"`
		`println(string1) // Prints "Hello world!"`
		`println(string4) // Prints "Hello world! Am I alone?"`
		`var string5 = string4`
		`let startIndex = advance(string5.startIndex, 13)`
		`string5.replaceRange(startIndex..<string5.endIndex, with: "How do you like me now?")`
		`if string4 != string5 {`
		`println(string5)`
		`}`
		`// Prints "Hello world! How do you like me now?"`

	`NSMutableString *tempHigh = [@"85" mutableCopy];`
	`NSMutableString *tempLow = [@"70" mutableCopy];`
	`NSString *degreeF = @"\u2109";`
	`[tempHigh appendString:degreeF];`
	`[tempLow appendString:degreeF];`
	`NSLog(@"High/Low: %@/%@", tempHigh, tempLow); // Prints "High/Low: 85°F/70°F"`
		`var tempHigh = "85"`
		`var tempLow = "70"`
		`let degreeF: Character = "\u{2109}"`
		`tempHigh.append(degreeF)`
		`tempLow.append("\u{2109}" as Character)`
		`println("High/Low: \(tempHigh)/\(tempLow)") // Prints "High/Low: 85°F/70°F"`

Creating Tuples and Collections

Swift defines two formal collection types: `Array` and `Dictionary`. Although collections of type `NSSet`, `NSMutableSet` and `NSCountedSet` can be created and worked with in Swift using `Foundation` API, there are no direct counterparts to these classes in the Swift standard library. Although not a formal collection type, Swift does add a new type for which there is no counterpart in Objective-C that can be used for grouping multiple values into a single compound value, called a *tuple*.

Creating Tuples

Tuples, although new to Objective-C developers transitioning to Swift, are by no means a new programming construct. Tuples can be found in several other languages, including Python, Haskell, and C#. Tuples in Swift are intended for temporarily grouping related values, and Apple advises to not use tuples to create complex data structures. Common uses include returning multiple values from a function (see Chapter 6 for details) and to test multiple values in a `switch case` statement (covered in Chapter 5). For data structures that are more complex or will persist beyond a temporary scope, use a class or structure instead (covered in Chapter 7).

Tuple values are ordered and can be composed of the same or differing types. To create a tuple, enclose a comma-separated list of values in parentheses:

```
var httpStatus = (200, "OK")
```

The previous example relies on type inference and the tuple created is of type `(Int, String)`. You can also explicitly state the type of a tuple, as in the following example, which adheres to good form by making the variable an optional, because we do not assign a value:

```
var httpStatus: (Int, String)?
```

Because tuples are ordered lists, you can access tuple elements at their numerical order index (beginning with 0) using dot syntax:

```
var httpStatus = (200, "OK")
let code = httpStatus.0
let message = httpStatus.1
println("The code is \(code) and the message is \(message).")
```

More succinctly, tuples can also be decomposed into separate stored values using another tuple:

```
let (code, message) = httpStatus
println("The code is \(code) and the description is \(message).")
```

You can also optionally assign a name to one or more tuple elements during creation, and subsequently access named elements by either name or index.

```
let httpStatus = (200, message: "OK")
println("The code is \(httpStatus.0) and the message is
\(httpStatus.message).")
```

If you do not need to access a tuple element during decomposition, you can ignore it by using an underscore character. You'll see similar usage elsewhere in Swift, generally encouraged to aid performance and code clarity:

```
let (code, _) = httpStatus
println("The code is \(code).")
```

Tuples can also be nested:

```
let (score, (firstName, _)) = (100, ("Scott", "Gardner"))
println("\(firstName) received a score of \(score).")
```

Table 3-2 demonstrates how tuples in Swift can reduce code and increase clarity, compared with how you might perform the same task in Objective-C.

***Table 3-2.** Comparing Objective-C and Swift tuple approach to performing a common task*

Objective-C	`NSUInteger code = 200;`
	`NSString *message = @"OK";`
	`NSLog(@"The code is %lu and the message is %@.",`
	`(unsigned long)code, message);`

Swift	`let (code, message) = (200, "OK")` `println("The code is \(code) and the message is \(message).")`

Creating Arrays

Like Objective-C, arrays in Swift store ordered collections of values in a zero-indexed list (i.e., the first item is at index 0). Unlike Objective-C, in which arrays can only store objects, Swift arrays can store values of any type, and as Apple's Swift language guide states repeatedly, an array should store values of the same type.

As with any variable or constant, a Swift array's type can be inferred based on its contents if set during declaration, or it can be explicitly stated. Swift's literal syntax for creating an array is the same as Objective-C's literal syntax but without the @ prefix.

Table 3-3 compares creating arrays in Objective-C and Swift. Notice the lack of using the `const` keyword in Objective-C, as doing so does not make the array any more immutable.

Table 3-3. *Creating arrays in Objective-C and Swift*

	Objective-C	Swift
Mutable array	`NSMutableArray *planets = [@[@"Mercury", @"Venus", @"Earth"] mutableCopy];`	`var planets = ["Mercury", "Venus", "Earth"]`
Immutable array	`NSArray *planets = @[@"Mercury", @"Venus"];`	`let planets = ["Mercury", "Venus"]`

> **Note** For what it's worth, `-[NSObject mutableCopy]` facilitates using a shorter syntax for creating a mutable array than using `+[NSMutableArray arrayWithObjects:]` in Objective-C, and performance is not noticeably different until about 2,000,000 iterations.

In the previous table, the Swift array type is inferred based on the type of the values stored in the array. A Swift array's type can also be explicity stated during declaration. The syntax for doing so is to enter the type enclosed in square brackets, or specify the type is of `Array<SomeType>`, although the former is preferred. Specifying an array is optional (using ? postfix) indicates that the array can be `nil`, in addition to being empty or containing values:

```
var intArray1: [Int] = [1, 2, 3]
var intArray2: Array<String>?
var intArray3: [Int]?
```

You can create an empty array using `Array`'s initializer syntax with either type declaration approach. Table 3-4 compares creating mutable empty arrays in Objective-C and Swift.

Table 3-4. Creating mutable empty arrays in Objective-C and Swift

Objective-C	Swift

`NSMutableArray *arrayOfAnyObjects = [NSMutableArray array];`	`var stringArray = Array<String>()`
	`var intArray = [Int]()`
	`var myClassArray = [MyClass]()`

> **Note** There are of course additional ways to instantiate an empty array in Objective-C, such as `[[NSMutableArray alloc] init]`, `[NSMutableArray new]`, and `[[NSMutableArray alloc] initWithCapacity:<#(NSUInteger)#>]`. Because our focus is on transitioning to and learning Swift, Objective-C examples will typically be a single common use-case versus being exhaustive.

It is possible to store different types in a Swift array; however, doing so may produce unexpected results with type inference. For example, an array of `Int`s and `String`s has its type inferred to be `NSArray`, but add an `NSObject` instance to it and its type is then inferred to be `[NSObject]`, and yet add an instance of a custom Swift reference type such as the `MyClass` type we created earlier, and the array's type is once again inferred to be `NSArray`. What should be mentioned, however, is that if you need an array that can hold multiple types, you can do so by explicitly declaring a variable array of type `[AnyClass]` or `[Any]`, the former being an array capable of holding any reference type, the latter capable of holding any type whatsoever; `AnyClass` is a `typealias` for `AnyObject`:

```
var anyArray = [Any]()
var anyClassArray = [AnyClass]()
```

Swift arrays also have an initializer to create an array of a specified `count` with each element having the specified `repeatedValue`:

```
var studentScores = [(String, Int)](count: 3, repeatedValue: ("Name", 100))
println(studentScores) // Prints "[(Name, 100), (Name, 100), (Name, 100)]"
```

Creating Dictionaries

Apple defines a Swift dictionary as being an unordered container that stores multiple values of the same type, wherein each value is associated with a unique identifier key.

Objective-C dictionaries can only store objects, and can use any object for the key as long as it conforms to the NSCopying protocol. Swift dictionaries can store any type and use any type for the key as long as it conforms to the Hashable protocol (protocols are covered in Chapter 8). All of Swift's basic value types can be used as dictionary keys, including Character, String, Int, Double, Float, and Bool. Also, members of a new type of enumeration in Swift (in which its members are not specifically assigned a value) can be used as dictionary keys (enumerations are covered in Chapter 7).

The literal syntax for creating a Swift dictionary uses square brackets just like arrays, and has the same key: value syntax as found in Objective-C's literal syntax, sans the @. Table 3-5 compares creating dictionaries in Objective-C and Swift.

***Table 3-5.** Creating dictionaries in Objective-C and Swift*

	Objective-C	Swift
Mutable dictionary	`NSMutableDictionary *planets = [@{@1: @"Mercury", @2: @"Venus", @3: @"Earth"} mutableCopy];`	`var planets = [1: "Mercury", 2: "Venus", 3: "Earth"]`
Immutable dictionary	`NSDictionary *planets = [@{@1: @"Mercury", @2: @"Venus", @3: @"Earth"} mutableCopy];`	`let planets = [1: "Mercury", 2: "Venus", 3: "Earth"]`

A Swift dictionary's type can be inferred by the type of keys and values assigned to the dictionary during declaration, as in the preceding table, or they can be explicitly stated during declaration using either literal [KeyType: ValueType] or full Dictionary<KeyType, ValueType> syntax, with the literal syntax being preferable:

```
var stringDictionary1: [Int: String] = [1: "One", 2: "Two"]
var stringDictionary2: Dictionary<Int, String>?
var stringDictionary3: [Int: String]?
```

You can create an empty dictionary using Dictionary's initializer syntax with either type declaration approach, or as may be commonly seen, by initially assigning a key/value pair (thereby relying on type inference to establish the key and value types) and then setting the dictionary to an empty dictionary ([:]). Table 3-6 compares creating mutable empty dictionaries in Objective-C and Swift.

Table 3-6. Creating mutable empty dictionaries in Objective-C and Swift

Objective-C	Swift

`NSMutableDictionary *dictionaryOfAnyObjects = [NSMutableDictionary dictionary];`	`var stringDictionary1 = [Int: String]()`
	`var stringDictionary2 = Dictionary<Int, String>()`
	`var stringDictionary3 = [1: ""]`
	`stringDictionary3 = [:]`

It is possible to create a dictionary in Swift that is assigned multiple types of keys and values during declaration; however, doing so not only changes the dictionary's type to `NSDictionary`, but it also makes the dictionary immutable. Although the Swift standard library does not enable you to declare a `Dictionary` type that uses different (hashable) key types and multiple value types (that is, `[Hashable: Any]` won't work), it does enable you to create a dictionary of a specified key type that can store multiple value types:

```
var dictionaryOfAnyTypes = [Int: Any]()
var dictionaryOfAnyClassTypes = [String: AnyClass]()
```

Mutability

Swift's approach to mutability of tuples and collections is logical and consistent, yet somewhat different from Objective-C. The next section will cover modifying tuples and collections. It is important first to gain a solid understanding of how mutability is applied to Swift tuples, arrays, and dictionaries.

As with all stored values in Swift, the mutability of a Swift tuple, array, or dictionary is determined during declaration, not by choice of class as it is in Objective-C (`NSArray`/`NSMutableArray`, `NSDictionary`/`NSMutableDictionary`).

Swift tuples and collections declared as variables can be reassigned to new tuples or collections, respectively, of the same type. Arrays and dictionaries–but not tuples–declared as variables can have items added to and removed from them. Arrays and dictionaries declared as constants cannot be reassigned, nor can they have items added or removed.

Mutability of the values within a tuple or collection is applied as follows. Value types passed into a tuple or collection are passed by copy, inheriting the mutability of the tuple or collection. So a variable or constant value type assigned to a variable tuple or passed in to a variable array is copied in as a mutable variable. Similarly, a variable or constant value type passed in as the value of a key/value pair to a constant dictionary is copied in as an immutable constant. Table 3-7 summarizes the mutability of tuples, arrays, and dictionaries in Objective-C and Swift.

Table 3-7. Summary of tuple, array, and dictionary mutability in Objective-C and Swift

	Tuple	Array	Dictionary
Objective-C			
Mutable	N/A	Values can be added or removed Values can be modified	Same as for Array
Immutable	N/A	Values cannot be added or removed Values can be modified	Same as for Array
Swift			
Variable	Value types are modifiable Variable properties of reference types are modifiable	Same as for Tuple, plus values can be added or removed	Same as for Tuple, plus values can be added or removed
Constant	Value types are not modifiable Variable properties of reference types are modifiable	Same as for Tuple	Same as for Tuple

Multidimensional Tuples and Collections

Swift tuples and collections can contain nested tuples and collections, just like arrays and dictionaries in Objective-C:

```
var tupleWithArrayWithTuplesAndDictionaryWithArrays = (([(1, 2, 3),
(4, 5, 6)]),[1: ["a", "b", "c"], 2: ["d", "e", "f", "g"]])
println(tupleWithArrayWithTuplesAndDictionaryWithArrays.0)
// Prints "[(1, 2, 3), (4, 5, 6)]"
println(tupleWithArrayWithTuplesAndDictionaryWithArrays.1)
// Prints "[1: [a, b, c], 2: [d, e, f, g]]"
println(tupleWithArrayWithTuplesAndDictionaryWithArrays.1[2]![3])
// Prints "g"
```

Working with Tuples and Collections

The following three subsections will cover most aspects of working with tuples, arrays, and dictionaries. Enumerating collections, due to the relationship of these use cases to controlling program flow, is deferred to Chapter 5.

Working with Tuples

A tuple cannot be sorted, nor can it have items added to or removed from it. A variable tuple can be modified, and its value type elements can also be modified. Use the same dot syntax to change the value of a tuple element as you would to access it, but each value can only be changed to a new value of the same type. Value types passed into a variable tuple can be modified, whereas value types passed into a constant tuple cannot. This is regardless of whether the value type being passed in is itself declared as a variable or constant, because—remember—value types are always passed by copy:

```
var spade = ("Spade", symbol: "♣")
let club = ("Club", symbol: "♠")
spade.symbol = "♠"
var suits = (spade: spade, club: club)
suits.club.symbol = "♣"
println(suits.club) // Prints "(Club, ♣ )"
println(club) // Prints "(Club, ♠ )"
```

Reference types are passed by reference, and therefore, their mutability—that is, the mutability of their properties—within a tuple is the same as outside the tuple (Chapter 7 will cover reference types in depth, including the syntax used to create the class in the following example):

```
class MyClass {
  var myVariableProperty = "Can be changed"
}

let myClass1 = MyClass()
let myClass2 = MyClass()
var classTuple = (myClass1, myClass2)
classTuple.0.myVariableProperty = "Changed"
```

A tuple can also be declared to store value types of `Any` (value or reference types) or `AnyClass` (reference types only), and subsequently have those members assigned and reassigned:

```
var suits: (Any, Any, Any, Any)
suits = ("Spade", "Club", "Heart", "Diamond")
suits.0 = ["Spade": "♠ "]
suits.1 = ["Club": "♣ "]
suits.2 = ["Heart": "♥ "]
suits.3 = ["Diamond": "♦ "]
```

Working with Arrays

Table 3-8 compares several ways to work with arrays in Objective-C and Swift, following highlights of the similarities and differences between the two.

Swift uses the same subscript syntax as Objective-C to access array items. NSArray instances have count, firstObject, and lastObject properties, and, similarly, Array values have count, first, and last computed properties. Ranges of items can be retrieved from Objective-C arrays using -[NSArray subarrayWithRange:], whereas Swift enables using *range operators* with subscript syntax to retrieve or replace a subarray of values from another array. When replacing a range of values, the replacement array does not need to be the same length as the range it is replacing. There are two kinds of range operators: the *closed range operator* (..., as in a...e) includes the range of values from the start value to and including the end value (a to and including e), and the *half-open range operator* (..<, as in a..<e) includes the range of values from the start value up to but *not* including the end value (a up to but not e). Range operators will be mentioned again in the next chapter on operators and receive additional coverage in Chapter 5 for their use in program control flow statements.

To check if an array is empty in Objective-C, the count property can be checked to see if it is greater than 0; however, Swift includes the isEmpty computed property for this purpose.

Finding items in an NSArray is made possible by a variety of indexOf... methods such as -[NSArray indexOfObject:], coupled with using subscript syntax or -[NSArray objectAtIndex:] to access the found item. Swift simplifies this task with the find() method, which searches the array passed in for the value passed in, and returns an optional wrapping the value if found, or nil if not. Pairing up with Objective-C's -[NSArray filteredArrayUsingPredicate:], which takes an NSPredicate instance, Swift includes includes a filter() method that takes a *closure* (similar to a block in Objective-C) that returns a Bool, which can be used to return an array matching the conditions of the filter. Closures are a powerful feature Swift with a variety of different usage syntax options. For completeness, examples of closure usage with arrays will be included in Table 3-8 using the most compact version of syntax possible. This syntax may seem slightly esoteric at first, but once understood by the community-at-large of Swift developers, it should quickly become the de facto standard. See Chapter 6 for elaborate coverage of closures and the variety of syntax options. One tip that may help make sense of the syntax in these examples before consulting Chapter 6 is that numbers prefixed with $ refer to a closure's arguments (e.g., $0 is the first argument).

Arrays can be sorted in Objective-C using a comparator block, selector, function, or descriptor. Swift array can be sorted using `sorted()` and `sort()` (the former returns a new array and the latter mutates the array it is called on), and also `map()` and `reduce()` methods, all of which take advantage of closures to reorder, transform, and combine an array's items, respectively.

Adding to and replacing items in an `NSMutableArray` instance in Objective-C can be done via methods that include `-[NSMutableArray addObject:]`, `-[NSMutableArray insertObjectAtIndex:]`, `-[NSMutableArray replaceObjectsAtIndexes:withObjects:]`, and variations. Similar methods are available for `Array` in Swift, and additionally, Swift enables use of the + and += operators to concatenate two arrays.

> **Note** A value itself cannot be added to a Swift array using the + and += operators. Use the `append()` method instead, or optionally enclose the value(s) in an array to use as the right operand of a + or += operator.

Removing items from an `NSMutableArray` instance in Objective-C is accomplished using a variety of `remove...` methods such as `-[NSMutableArray removeObjectAtIndex:]`. Swift matches these methods with `removeAtIndex()` and others.

Table 3-8 includes setup code at the top for use in the examples that follow.

***Table 3-8.** Comparing Objective-C `NSArray` and `NSMutableArray` methods and techniques to Swift `Array` equivalents*

	Objective-C	Swift
	`NSMutableArray *array = [@[@1, @2, @3, @4, @5] mutableCopy];`	`var array = [1, 2, 3, 4, 5]`

Inspect	`NSLog(@"array is empty? %@", array.count ? @"NO" : @"YES");`
	`// Prints "NO"`
	`NSLog(@"%lu", (unsigned long) array.count); // Prints "5"`
		`println(array.isEmpty)`
		`// Prints "false"`
		`println(array.count)`
		`// Prints "5"`

Access	`NSNumber *itemAtIndex3 = array[3]; // 4`
	`NSArray *rangeOf0to3 = [array subarrayWithRange:NSMakeRange (0, 3)]; // (1, 2, 3)`
	`NSArray *rangeOf0through3 = [array subarrayWithRange: NSMakeRange(0, 4)]; // (1, 2, 3, 4)`
		`let itemAtIndex3 = array[3] // 4`
		`let rangeOf0to3 = array[0..<3] // [1, 2, 3]`
		`let rangeOf0through3 = array[0...3] // [1, 2, 3, 4]`

Find	`NSInteger index = [array indexOfObject:@5];` `NSNumber *foundItem = array[index]; // 5`	`let foundItem = find(array, 5)! // 4`

Filter	`NSPredicate *predicate = [NSPredicate predicateWithFormat:@"self > 3"];`
	`NSArray *greaterThan3 = [array filt eredArrayUsingPredicate:predicate];`
	`// (4, 5)`
		`let greaterThan5 = array.filter { $0 > 3 }`
		`// [4, 5]`

Sort	`NSSortDescriptor *descriptor = [NSSortDescriptor sortDescriptorWithKey:@"self" ascending:NO];`
	`NSArray * reverseSortedArray = [[array sortedArrayUsingDescriptors: @[descriptor]] mutableCopy];`
	`// (5, 4, 3, 2, 1)`
		`let reverseSortedArray = sorted(array, >) // [5, 4, 3, 2, 1]`
		`array.sort { $0 > $1 }`
		`// [5, 4, 3, 2, 1]`

Append	`[array addObject:@7]; // (1, 2, 3, 4, 5, 7)`	`array = [1, 2, 3, 4, 5]`
		`array += [7] // [1, 2, 3, 4, 5, 7]`
		`// array.append(7) could also have been used`

(continued)

Table 3-8. (*continued*)

	Objective-C	Swift
Insert	`[array insertObject:@0 atIndex:0];` `// (0, 1, 2, 3, 4, 5, 7)`	`array.insert(0, atIndex: 0)` `// [0, 1, 2, 3, 4, 5, 7]`
Replace	`array[6] = @6; // (0, 1, 2, 3, 4, 5, 6)`	`array[6] = 6 // [0, 1, 2, 3, 4, 5, 6]`
Remove	`[array removeLastObject];` `// (0, 1, 2, 3, 4, 5)`	`array.removeLast()` `// [0, 1, 2, 3, 4, 5]`

Map	`NSMutableArray *dollarsArray = [NSMutableArray array];`
	`[array enumerateObjectsUsingBlock: ^(id obj, NSUInteger idx, BOOL *stop) {`
	`[dollarsArray addObject:[NSString stringWithFormat:@"%@%@", @"$", obj]];`
	`}];`
	`NSLog(@"%@", dollarsArray);`
	`// Prints "("$0", "$1", "$2", "$3", "$4", "$5")"`
		`let dollarsArray = array.map { "$\($0)" } // ["$0", "$1", "$2", "$3", "$4", "$5"]`

Reduce	`int totalOfArray;`
	`for (NSNumber *i in array) {`
	`totalOfArray += [i intValue];`
	`}`
	`NSLog(@"%i", totalOfArray);`
	`// Prints "15"`
		`let totalOfArray = array.reduce(0, +) // 15`

Working with Dictionaries

Objective-C and Swift dictionaries work in similar ways, yet have some differences that will be noted first, followed by comparative examples in Table 3-9.

Swift dictionaries have `isEmpty` and `count` computed properties just like arrays, the latter of which is also available in Objective-C as a property of `NSDictionary` and `NSMutableDictionary` instances.

Objective-C's `-[NSDictionary allKeys]` and `-[NSDictionary allValues]` methods that return `NSArray` instances (order unspecified) have corresponding `keys` and `values` computed properties for Swift dictionaries. The return value for these computed properties in Swift, however, is of a collection type that can be enumerated just like a regular array (see chapter 5 for details), or new arrays can be created from the collections using syntax that will be demonstrated in Table 3-9. The collections returned for both the keys and values computed properties are ordered ascending by key, as is the order of key-value pairs when a Dictionary value is printed out.

Swift uses the same subscript syntax as Objective-C to access dictionary items. Values can be retrieved and added using subscript syntax in both Objective-C and Swift. Retrieving a value from a Swift dictionary is handled differently. Because a lookup may not find a value for the key provided, the returned value is an optional of the value if found, or nil if not. Similar to -[NSMutableDictionary setObject:forKey:] in Objective-C (and -[NSMutableDictionary setValue:forKey:], except that it requires an NSString instance for the key), Swift dictionary values can also be changed using the updateValue(forKey:) method. Unlike in Objective-C, however, updateValue(forKey:) returns an optional of the old value, and if a value was not found for the key provided, a new value for that key is added and nil is returned.

Although Objective-C does not allow it, a key-value pair can be removed from a Swift Dictionary type by using subscript syntax to set the value to nil for the key. Both languages offer methods to remove items by key or remove all items; however, Swift does not currently offer a counterpart to Objective-C's -[NSMutableDictionary removeObjectsForKeys:].

***Table 3-9.** Comparing Objective-C NSDictionary and NSMutableDictionary methods and techniques to Swift Dictionary equivalents*

	Objective-C	Swift
	NSMutableDictionary *dictionary = [@{@1: @"One", @2: @"Two", @3: @"Three"} mutableCopy];	var dictionary = [1: "One", 2: "Two", 3: "Three"]

Inspect	NSLog(@"%@", dictionary.count ? @"NO" : @"YES"); // Prints "NO"
	NSLog(@"%lu", (unsigned long) dictionary.count); // Prints "3"
		println(dictionary.isEmpty) // Prints "false"
		println(dictionary.count) // Prints "3"

Access	NSLog(@"%@", dictionary[@1]); // Prints "One"
	NSArray *dictionaryKeys = [dictionary allKeys]; // (3, 1, 2)
	NSArray *dictionaryValues = [dictionary allValues]; // (Three, One, Two)
		println(dictionary[1]) // Prints "One"
		let dictionaryKeys = [Int] (dictionary.keys) // [1, 2, 3]
		let dictionaryValues = [String] (dictionary.values) // ["One", "Two", "Three"]

(continued)

Table 3-9. (*continued*)

	Objective-C	Swift

Insert	`dictionary[@4] = @"Five";`
	`NSLog(@"%@", dictionary);`
	`// Prints "(3 = Three, 2 = Two, 1 = One, 4 = Five)"`
		`dictionary[4] = "Five"`
		`println(dictionary) // Prints "[1: One, 2: Two, 3: Three, 4: Five]"`

Update	`dictionary[@4] = @"Four";`
	`// (3 = Three, 2 = Two, 1 = One, 4 = Four)`
		`dictionary[4] = "Six"`
		`// [1: "One", 2: "Two", 3: "Three", 4: "Six"]`
		`if let oldValue = dictionary.updateValue("Four", forKey: 4) {`
		`println("The value for key 4 was changed from \(oldValue) to \(dictionary[4]!)")`
		`}`
		`// Prints "The value for key 4 was changed from Six to Four"`

Remove	`[dictionary removeObjectForKey:@4];`
	`NSLog(@"%@", dictionary);`
	`// Prints "(3 = Three, 2 = Two, 1 = One)"`
		`dictionary[4] = nil`
		`println(dictionary) // Prints "[1: One, 2: Two, 3: Three]"`

Syntax Reference

Figures 3-1 to 3-5 provide syntax summaries for creating characters, strings, tuples, arrays, and dictionaries in Swift. The same optional declarations (? and !) can be used as demonstrated in the variable and constant syntax summary in Figure 2-3 (see Chapter 2), and are thus omitted here. Italicized text indicates optional components, which are omitted in successive examples of identical usage for each type.

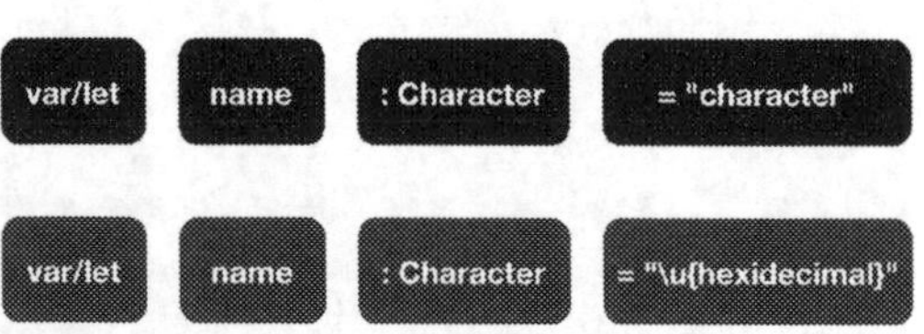

Figure 3-1. *Syntax for creating characters in Swift*

var
name
: String
= ""
var
name
= String()
var/let
name
= "text"
var/let
name
= "... \(expression) ..."
var/let
name
= String("format", argument, ...)
var/let
name
= String("format", [argument, ...])

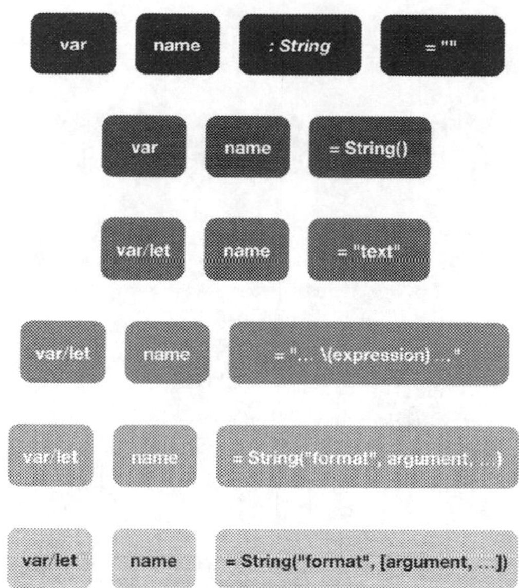

Figure 3-2. *Syntax for creating strings in Swift*

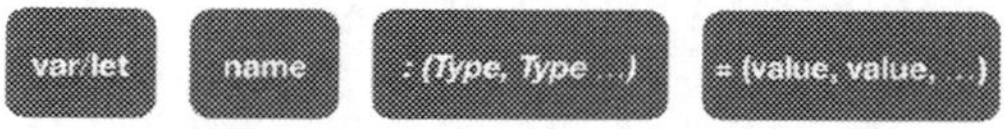

var/let
name
: (Type, Type ...)
= (value, value, ...)

Figure 3-3. *Syntax for creating tuples in Swift*

var/let
name
: [Type]
= [value, ...]
var/let
name
: Array<Type>
= [value, ...]
var
name
= [Type]()
var
name
= Array<Type>()

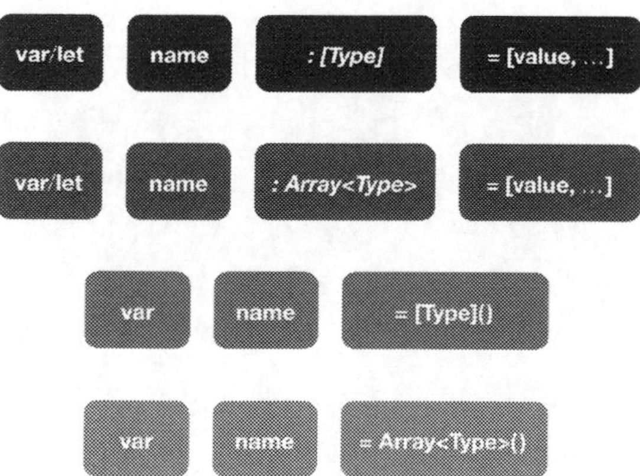

Figure 3-4. *Syntax for creating arrays in Swift*

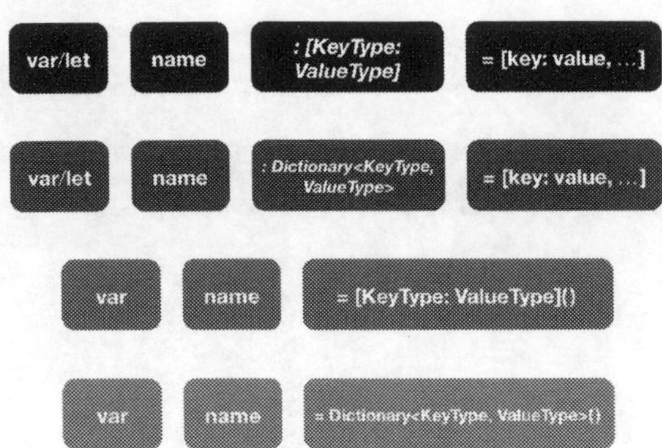

***Figure 3-5.** Syntax for creating dictionaries in Swift*

Summary

In this chapter you learned how to create and work with strings and collections in Swift, as compared with performing these tasks in Objective-C. Although there are many similarities between the two languages, it is important to not only understand the syntactic differences but also to strive toward taking full advantage of the powerful new capabilities provided in Swift.

Chapter 4

Performing Operations

This chapter will focus on performing operations, including arithmetic, logical, bitwise, type checking, and type casting. Operator precedence and associativity rules will also be reviewed.

Basic Operators

Swift includes the same basic operators as Objective-C, yet it adheres to a slightly different set of rules for operator precedence and associativity that are intended to be simpler and more predictable. Precedence and associativity will be covered later in this chapter.

The basic operators are implemented in Swift in the same manner as Objective-C, with a few exceptions and additions that will be mentioned next, followed by a summary of all basic operators with examples in Tables 4-1 through 4-4.

In both Objective-C and Swift, `==` and `!=` operators test for value equality (or inequality) for number values (`NSInteger`, `NSUInteger`, `NSNumber`, etc. in Objective-C; `Int`, `UInt`, etc. in Swift). For objects (`NSObject` and subclasses) in Objective-C and reference types in Swift, `==` and `!=` test that the objects/reference types are the same identical thing – same hash value – or are not the same identical thing, respectively. Custom reference types do not automatically implement these *equal to* operators; see Chapter 7 for details.

These *equal to* operators are also not implemented for other types such as structures in either language. However, custom operators can be created in Swift, and existing operators can be overloaded. Creating custom operators and overloading existing operators will be covered in Chapter 6.

Swift also introduces two new *identity equality* operators (=== and !==), which check referential equality of reference types (and thus could have been called *referential equality* operators). These operators automatically apply to custom reference types, too.

The + operator is used in Objective-C to add scalar numbers (including typedefs such as NSInteger). Similarly, + is used in Swift to add two number value types. As was covered in the last chapter, the + operator can also be used to concatenate two values of type String or type Array, and it can be used to concatenate two Character types to create a String type.

The += operator can be used in Objective-C with scalar numbers and associated typedefs as shorthand syntax to combine addition and assignment (a += b is the same as a = a + b). The += operator is used in the same way in Swift with number value types, and, as explained in the last chapter, it can be used to concatenate and assign two values of type String or Array, but not Character (because the resulting String type is not assignable to a Character type).

The % operator, known as the *modulo operator* in Objective-C, is referred to in Swift as the *remainder operator*. Swift expands usage of the remainder operator to include floating-point numbers.

In Objective-C, value overflow and underflow is automatic, which can result in unexpected behavior and sometimes hard-to-find bugs. For example, if you create 8-bit integer (of which maximum value is 255) and attempt to add 1 to that value, it will overflow and essentially "wrap around" to the value 0. As part of Swift's "safe by design" credo, overflow and underflow conditions will result in a compile-time error by default, versus creating an invalid or unexpected value during runtime. However, you can opt in to overflow/underflow handling in Swift by using the overflow operators for addition (&+), subtraction (&-), multiplication (&*), division (&/), and remainder (&%), in place of the regular operators.

Note When using an overflow operator, the first operand is referenced to determine legality of assignment before the operation is performed, instead of the result of the whole operation.

Along similar lines, division by 0 or calculating modulo 0 in Objective-C will return 0. In Swift, either attempt will result in a compile-time error unless you use the equivalent overflow operator, in which case 0 will be returned just like in Objective-C.

Swift adds a new *nil coalescing operator* (??) for use with optionals. This operator provides a shorthand syntax alternative to using a ternary conditional operator.

Although the ternary conditional operator (?:) is implemented the same way in both languages, it should be pointed out that nonoptional values in Swift cannot be checked in a boolean manner such as in Objective-C. In Swift, it is necessary to explicitly check if a nonoptional variable does not equal nil (!= nil) in a ternary conditional operator, or in other conditional checks, as you'll see in the next chapter.

There are two more new Swift operators: the *closed range operator* (..., as in a...e) and *half-open range operator* (..<, as in a..<e). Because these operators are predominantly used in controlling program flow, they will be covered in the next chapter, focused entirely on that topic.

Unary operators operate on a single target, binary on two targets, and ternary on three targets. Tables 4-1 through 4-4 summarize the basic operators found in Objective-C and Swift. For Swift's overflow operators (that do not exist in Objective-C), comparable examples from Objective-C are provided.

***Table 4-1.** Comparison operators in Objective-C and Swift*

	Objective-C	Swift

	`NSInteger a = 4;`
	`NSInteger b = 2;`
	`NSObject *x = [NSObject new];`
	`NSObject *y = [NSObject new];`
	`NSObject *z = x;`
		`let a = 4`
		`let b = 2`
		`let x = NSObject()`
		`let y = NSObject()`
		`let z = x`

==	`a == b // False`
	`x == y // False`
	`x == z // True`
		`a == b // False`
		`x == y // False`
		`x == z // True`

!=	`a != b // True` `x != y // True`	`a != b // True`
>	`a > b // True`	`a > b // True`
<	`a < b // False`	`a < b // False`
>=	`a >= (b * b) // True`	`a >= (b * b) // True`
<=	`a <= (b * b) // True`	`a <= (b * b) // True`
===	N/A	`x === z // True`
!==	N/A	`x !== y // True`

Table 4-2. Basic unary operators in Objective-C and Swift

	Objective-C	Swift
	NSInteger a = 1;	var a = 1

++	NSInteger b = ++a;
	// b = 2, a = 2
	NSInteger c = a++;
	// c = 2, a = 3
		let b = ++a
		// b = 2, a = 2
		let c = a++
		// c = 2, a = 3

--	NSInteger d = a--;
	// d = 3, a = 2
	NSInteger e = --a;
	// e = 1, a = 1
		let d = a--
		// d = 3, a = 2
		let e = --a
		// e = 1, a = 1

Table 4-3. Basic binary operators in Objective-C and Swift

	Objective-C	Swift

	NSInteger a = 7;
	NSInteger b = 3;
	uint8_t g = 255;
	uint8_t h = 0;
		var a = 7
		let b = 3
		var c = "Hello "
		let d = "🌎"
		let e = [1, 2, 3]
		let f = [4, 5, 6]
		let g = UInt8.max
		let h = UInt8.min

+	NSInteger i = a + b;
	// i = 10
		let i = a + b
		// i = 10
		let j = c + d
		// j = "Hello 🌎"
		var k = e + f
		// k = [1, 2, 3, 4, 5, 6]

+=	a += 1 // a = 8	a += 1 // a = 8 c += d // c = "Hello 🌎" k += [7] // k = [1, 2, 3, 4, 5, 6, 7]

-, -=	NSInteger l = a - b;
	// l = 5
	l -= b; // l = 2
		var l = a - b
		// l = 5
		l -= b // l = 2

*, *=	NSInteger m = a * b;
	// m = 24
	m *= b; // k = 72
		var m = a * b
		// m = 24
		m *= b // k = 72

(continued)

Table 4-3. (*continued*)

	Objective-C	Swift

/, /=	NSInteger n = 10 / 4;
	// n = 2
	n /= 2; // l = 1
	CGFloat o = 10 / 4.0f;
	// o = 2.5
		var n = 10 / 4
		// n = 2
		n /= 2 // n = 1
		let o = 10 / 4.0
		// o = 2.5 (o is inferred to be a Double)
		let p: Int = 10 / 4.0
		// p = 2

%	NSInteger q = 10 % 4;
	// q = 2
	NSInteger r = -10 % 4;
	// r = -2
	NSInteger s = 10 % -4;
	// s = 2
	NSInteger t = -10 % -4;
	// t = -2
		let q = 10 % 4
		// q = 2
		let r = -10 % 4
		// r = -2
		let s = 10 % -4
		// s = 2
		let t = -10 % -4
		// t = -2
		let u = 10 % 4.0
		// u = 2.0
		let v = 10.5 % 4.5
		// v = 1.5

&+	uint8_t w = g + 1; // w = 0	let w = g &+ 1 // w = 0
&-	uint8_t x = h - 1; // x = 255	let x = h &- 1 // x = 255
&*	uint8_t y = g * 2; // y = 254	let y = g &* 2 // y = 254
&/	uint8_t z = a / 0; // Division by zero is undefined	let z = a &/ 0 // z = 0
&%	uint8_t aa = 255 % 0; // Remainder by zero is undefined	let aa = 255 &% 0 // aa = 0
??	N/A	let defaultSize = "M" var selectedSize: String? let orderSize = selectedSize ?? defaultSize // orderSize = "M"

Table 4-4. Ternary conditional operators in Objective-C and Swift

	Objective-C	Swift
	`NSInteger a = 0;`	`let a = 0`

?:	`NSInteger b = a ? a : 5;`
	`// b = 5`
	`NSInteger c = a ?: 5;`
	`// c = 5`
		`let b = a != nil ? a : 5`
		`// b = 5`

Logical Operators

Swift implements the three standard logical operators in the same way as Objective-C. The *logical NOT operator* (!) inverts a boolean value. In Objective-C, you may have also been used to using the NOT operator to check that a nonboolean variable is not `nil`.

```
[NSURLConnection sendAsynchronousRequest:request queue:queue
completionHandler:^(NSURLResponse *response, NSData *data, NSError
*connectionError) {
  if (!error) {
    // ...
  }
}];
```

As will be further explained in the next chapter on controlling program flow, a regular (nonoptional) variable or constant in Swift cannot be checked for existence in a boolean manner.

The *logical AND operator* (&&) returns a boolean `true` if both expressions are true, and the *logical OR operator* (||) returns a boolean `true` if either expression is true. Both && and || short-circuit, such that if the first expression is false in the case of && or true in the case of ||, the second is not evaluated. It may therefore benefit performance to place more computationally expensive expressions to the right of simpler expressions. Logical operators are evaluated left to right, so use parentheses to group expressions and specify order of evaluation. And, generally, the use of parentheses is encouraged whenever it will help improve readability.

```
let levelCompleted = (defeatedEnemy && savedPrincess) || enteredCheatCode
```

Logical operators in Objective-C and Swift are summarized in Table 4-5.

Table 4-5. Logical operators in Objective-C and Swift

	Objective-C	Swift

	`BOOL warmOutside = NO;`
	`BOOL raining = NO;`
	`BOOL sunny = YES;`
		`let warmOutside = false`
		`let raining = false`
		`let sunny = true`

!	`BOOL bringAJacket = !warmOutside;` `// bringAJacket = YES`	`let bringAJacket = !warmOutside` `// bringAJacket = true`

&&	`BOOL goSwimming = sunny &&`
	`warmOutside;`
	`// goSwimming = NO`
		`let goSwimming = sunny &&`
		`warmOutside`
		`// goSwimming = false`

||	`BOOL seeMovie = !warmOutside ||`
	`raining;`
	`// seeMovie = YES`
		`let seeMovie = !warmOutside ||`
		`raining`
		`// seeMovie = true`

Bitwise Operators

Bitwise operators enable lower-level programming capabilities typically reserved for manipulating raw data. Swift supports all of the bitwise operators available in Objective-C. An in-depth discussion of performing bitwise operations is beyond the scope of this book; however, the examples in Table 4-6 should be sufficient to match these operations between Objective-C and Swift. Observe also that each bitwise shift left or right doubles or halves the value using overflow operators, that is, &* 2 and &/ 2 in Swift, respectively.

Table 4-6. Bitwise operations in Objective-C and Swift

		Objective-C	Swift

		`uint8_t a = 15;`
		`// a = 00001111`
		`uint8_t b = 252;`
		`// b = 11111100`
		`uint8_t c = 63;`
		`// c = 00111111`
			`let a: UInt8 = 15`
			`// a = 00001111`
			`let b: UInt8 = 252`
			`// b = 11111100`
			`let c: UInt8 = 63`
			`// c = 00111111`

~	NOT - inverts bits	`uint8_t d = ~a;` `// d = 240 = 11110000`	`let d = ~a` `// d = 240 = 11110000`
&	AND - compares bits and returns new number with 1s for matching bits and 0s for nonmatching bits	`uint8_t e = b & c;` `// e = 60 = 00111100`	`let e = b & c` `// d = 60 = 00111100`

(*continued*)

Table 4-6. (*continued*)

		Objective-C	Swift
|	OR - compares bits and returns new number with 1s for 1s in either number and 0s otherwise	`uint8_t f = b | c;` `// f = 255 = 11111111`	`let f = b | c` `// f = 255 = 11111111`
^	XOR - compares bits and returns new number with 0s for matching bits and 1s for nonmatching bits	`uint8_t g = b ^ c;` `// g = 195 = 11000011`	`let g = b ^ c` `// g = 195 = 11000011`
<<	Bitwise left shift	`uint8_t h = b << 1;` `// h = 248 = b * 2 = 11111000`	`let h = b << 1` `// h = 248 = b &* 2 = 11111000`
>>	Bitwise right shift	`uint8_t i = b >> 1;` `// i = 126 = b / 2 = 01111110`	`let i = b >> 1` `// i = 126 = b &/ 2 = 01111110`

Shorthand assignment syntax is also available for each of the bitwise binary operators in Swift, just as in Objective-C. For example, a &= b is equivalent to a = a & b.

Advanced Operators

The advanced operators covered in this section include the is and as operators, and the pattern matching operator (~=). As in the Basic Operators section, these operators will be introduced narratively with mention of important points relative to their counterpart operators or operations in Objective-C, followed by a summary of examples in Table 4-7; the if conditional syntax used will be covered in the next chapter.

Checking if an object is of a certain class type in Objective-C involves calling two NSObject methods: -[NSObject isKindOfClass:] and +[NSObject class]. Casting an object to a subclass is accomplished by prepending the instance with the subclass name in parentheses, which subsequently allows treating that object as the casted subclass. Because the actual object of its original type is actually returned, however, it is necessary to call `-[NSObject isKindOfClass:]` or `-[NSObject respondsToSelector:]` before calling a method of that casted subclass, in order to avoid a potential runtime exception if the cast was not successful.

Type checking and type casting are performed in Swift via the `is` and `as` operators, respectively. The `is` operator returns `true` if the stored value being checked is an instance of the specified type (or a subclass in the case of class types), or `false` if not. The `as` operator will return an instance of the casted type if successful. For class types, when a stored value being presented as of a specific class type is actually an instance of a subclass, the `as` operator will force downcast that instance to the subclass type. However, if the stored value is not actually an instance of the casted type (or a subclass in the case of class types), the downcast will fail at runtime and a runtime error will be triggered. Therefore, the `as?` operator should be used when it is not certain that the item being casted is actually an instance of the casted type (or a subclass for class types). The `as?` operator will always return an optional value, which will either be the casted instance, or `nil` if the cast fails. However, the compiler will flag an error and thus prevent writing code that attempts to explicitly cast to a type that the stored value is not an actual instance of (or a subclass of in the case of class types). Casting a value does not change the value in any way. For class types, full access to the properties and methods of the downcasted class type will only be available for the scope of the cast. The type checking and casting examples in Table 4-7 include empty class, subclass, and structure definitions, and program control flow statements necessary to demonstrate these concepts. Control flow statements are covered in Chapter 5 classes and structures in Chapter 7, and subclasses in Chapter 9.

Swift introduces the ability to overload an operator, and perhaps one of the most useful examples of this capability is the *pattern matching operator* (~=). By default, ~= simply compares two values using the == operator. The pattern matching operator is included here, complete with setup code, however, coverage of that setup code (which involves creating a function to overload the ~= operator) is deferred to Chapter 6.

Table 4-7. Advanced operations in Objective-C and Swift

<table>
<tr><th></th><th>Objective-C</th><th>Swift</th></tr>
<tr><td></td><td><pre>// In MyCustomClass.h
@import Foundation;
@interface ParentClass : NSObject
@end
@interface Subclass : ParentClass
@end
@interface SomeOtherClass : NSObject
@end
// In MyCustomClass.m
@implementation ParentClass
@end
@implementation Subclass
@end
@implementation SomeOtherClass
@end
// In -[AnotherClass someMethod] in
AnotherClass.m
NSArray *arrayOfClassInstances =
@[[ParentClass new], [Subclass new],
[SomeOtherClass new]];</pre></td><td><pre>struct StructA { }
struct StructB { }
let arrayOfStructureInstances:
[Any] = [StructA(), StructB()]
class ParentClass { }
class Subclass: ParentClass
{ }
class SomeOtherClass { }
let arrayOfClassInstances =
[ParentClass(), Subclass(),
SomeOtherClass()]
func ~= (string: String,
integer: Int) -> Bool {
    return string == "\(integer)"
}</pre></td></tr>
<tr><td>is</td><td><pre>// In -[AnotherClass someMethod] in
AnotherClass.m
for (id value in
arrayOfClassInstances) {
   if ([value isKindOfClass:
   [ParentClass class]]) {
     NSLog(@"%@", NSStringFromClass
     ([value class]));
   } else {
     NSLog(@"Not an instance of
     Subclass or ParentClass");
   }
}
/* Prints:
ParentClass
Subclass
Not an instance of Subclass or
ParentClass
*/</pre></td><td><pre>for value in
arrayOfStructureInstances {
   if value is StructA {
     println(_stdlib_
     getDemangledTypeName
     (value))
   } else {
     println("Not an instance
     of StructA")
   }
}
/* Prints:
...StructA
Not an instance of StructA
*/</pre></td></tr>
</table>

(*continued*)

Table 4-7. (*continued*)

	Objective-C	Swift

as	// In -[AnotherClass someMethod] in AnotherClass.m
	for (id value in arrayOfClassInstances) {
	   Subclass *item = (Subclass *)value;
	   if ([item isKindOfClass:[Subclass class]]) {
	     NSLog(@"%@", NSStringFromClass([item class]));
	   } else {
	     NSLog(@"Not an instance of Subclass");
	   }
	}
	/* Prints:
	Not an instance of Subclass
	Subclass
	Not an instance of Subclass
	*/
		for value in arrayOfClassInstances {
		   if value is Subclass {
		     let item = value as Subclass
		     println(_stdlib_getDemangledTypeName(item))
		   } else {
		     println("Not an instance of Subclass")
		   }
		}
		/* Prints:
		Not an instance of Subclass
		...Subclass
		Not an instance of Subclass
		*/

as?	N/A	for value in arrayOfClassInstances {
		   if let item = value as? ParentClass {
		     println(_stdlib_getDemangledTypeName(item))
		   } else {
		     println("Not an instance of ParentClass or a subclass")
		   }
		}
		/* Prints:
		...ParentClass
		...ParentClass
		Not an instance of ParentClass or a subclass
		*/

~=	N/A	let equal = "1" ~= 1 // equal = true

Operator Precedence and Associativity

Precedence rules apply when an expression contains two or more binary operators and parentheses are not used to group and explicitly specify the order in which operations should be performed. Associativity rules group these operations in a left-to-right or right-to-left fashion based on the operator type. A general best practice when dealing with a complex arithmetic expression is to always use parentheses; this not only helps to ensure intended precedence and associativity, but it also clearly conveys your intentions.

Table 4-8 compares operator precedence and associativity rules in Objective-C and Swift. Objective-C's operator precedence is typically presented ordinally from 1st (most precedent) to 16th (least precedent). However, Swift's precedence levels are cardinal, that is, the higher the number, the higher the precedence. So, for the benefit of comparison, Objective-C's ordinal order of precedence is converted into a cardinal score (e.g., 1st becomes a score of 16, and 16th becomes a score of 1). Also notice that Swift precedence levels are a factor of 10 as compared with Objective-C, presumably giving Apple leeway to insert new precedence/associativity levels in the future.

***Table 4-8.** Binary operator precedence (and associativity) classifications in Objective-C and Swift*

		Swift	Objective-C
<<	Bitwise left shift	160 (None)	11 (Left)
>>	Bitwise left right	160 (None)	11 (Left)
*	Multiply	150 (Left)	13 (Left)
/	Divide	150 (Left)	13 (Left)
%	Remainder (modulo in Objective-C)	150 (Left)	13 (Left)
&*	Overflow multiply	150 (Left)	N/A
&/	Overflow divide	150 (Left)	N/A
&%	Overflow remainder	150 (Left)	N/A
&	Bitwise AND	150 (Left)	8 (Left)
+	Add	140 (Left)	12 (Left)
-	Subtract	140 (Left)	12 (Left)
&+	Overflow add	140 (Left)	N/A
&-	Overflow subtract	140 (Left)	N/A
|	Bitwise OR	140 (Left)	6 (Left)

(*continued*)

Table 4-8. (*continued*)

		Swift	Objective-C
^	Bitwise XOR	140 (Left)	7 (Left)
..<	Half-open range	135 (None)	N/A
...	Closed range	135 (None)	N/A
is	Type check	132 (None)	N/A
as	Type cast	132 (None)	N/A
<	Less than	130 (None)	10 (Left)
<=	Less than or equal	130 (None)	10 (Left)
>	Greater than	130 (None)	10 (Left)
>=	Greater than or equal	130 (None)	10 (Left)
==	Equal	130 (None)	9 (Left)
!=	Not equal	130 (None)	9 (Left)
===	Identical	130 (None)	N/A
!==	Not identical	130 (None)	N/A
~=	Pattern match	130 (None)	N/A
&&	Logical AND	120 (Left)	5 (Left)
||	Logical OR	110 (Left)	4 (Left)
??	Nil coalescing	110 (Right)	N/A
?:	Ternary conditional	100 (Right)	3 (Right)
=	Assign	90 (Right)	2 (Right)
*=	Multiply and assign	90 (Right)	2 (Right)
/=	Divide and assign	90 (Right)	2 (Right)
%=	Remainder and assign	90 (Right)	2 (Right)
+=	Add and assign	90 (Right)	2 (Right)
-=	Subtract and assign	90 (Right)	2 (Right)
<<=	Bitwise left shift and assign	90 (Right)	2 (Right)
>>=	Bitwise right shift and assign	90 (Right)	2 (Right)
&=	Bitwise AND and assign	90 (Right)	2 (Right)
^=	Bitwise XOR and assign	90 (Right)	2 (Right)
|=	Bitwise OR and assign	90 (Right)	2 (Right)

> **Tip** Due to the differences in precedence between Objective-C and Swift operators, be careful when migrating Objective-C code to Swift to ensure that arithmetic expressions perform the intended calculations.

Behind the scenes, Swift transforms a nonparenthesized expression made up of multiple operators from a flat list of operands and operators into a tree made up of parenthesized subexpressions based on operator precedence and associativity.

```
let a: Double = 1 + 2 * 3 / 4 % 5 // Flat list: 1, +, 2, *, 3, /, 4, %, 5
// Transformed into tree (1 + (((2 * 3) / 4) % 5))
// a = 1 + ((6 / 4) % 5) = 1 + (1.5 % 5) = 1 + 1.5 = 2.5
```

In the previous example, the + operator is lower precedence to *, /, and %, which are all of the same precedence and left-associative. Figure 4-1 presents this visually as a binary expression tree.

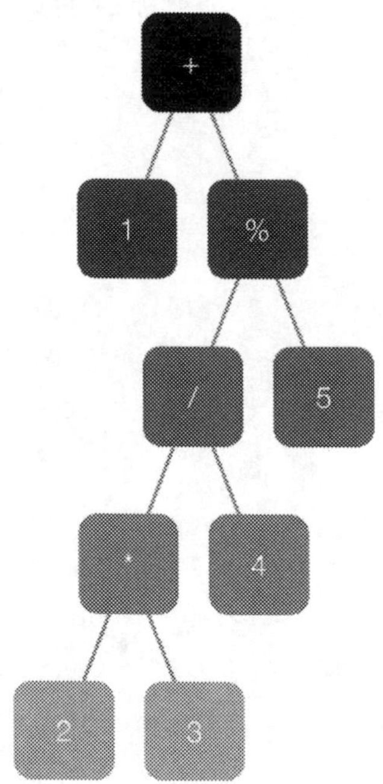

***Figure 4-1.** Binary expression tree representing the expression* `1 + 2 * 3 / 4 % 5`

Understanding how Swift transforms flat expressions into trees is of lesser importance when parentheses are used to explicity group expressions.

Summary

As demonstrated in this chapter, operators in Swift facilitate performing a wide variety of operations, including doing math, checking equality, changing types, and shifting bits. Although operator precedence will logically be applied to flat expressions, it is always better to use parentheses to control order of operator execution and improve code readability.

Chapter 5

Controlling Program Flow

Although there can be a multitude of ways in which to control program flow in code, often the best approach balances succinctness and readability with performance.

In this chapter, the similarities and differences of each control flow construct in Objective-C and Swift will be examined, and entirely new capabilities in Swift will be introduced.

Let's begin by covering two new Swift mechanisms for creating representations of iterable sequences that can be used in control flow statements: `range operators` and `stride()` functions.

Range Operators

Objective-C includes `NSRange`, which is a `struct` representing the `location` and `length` index of a series of values. Although it can be used outright to iterate over a range of `NSUIntegers` (from `range.location` to `range.length`), a `for` loop statement more succinctly serves the same purpose, and thus `NSRange`'s primary use is for creating or iterating over a subset portion of a series of values, such as characters in an `NSString` or objects in an `NSArray`. `NSRange` will be compared by example to Swift's range operators in Table 5-4 in the section Iteration and Enumeration.

Swift offers two range operators that enable expressing and iterating over a range of index values: the *closed range operator* (`...`, as in `a...e`) and *half-open range operator* (`..<`, as in `a..<e`). Both operators include a start value, an end value, and a generator to return each incremental value from the start value to each incremental value up to and including the end value in the case of the closed range operator, and up to but not including the end value in the case of the half-open range operator. A range operator's start value must be less than or equal to its end value, keeping in mind that

a closed operator with the same start and end values represents a range of one value (the end value), and a half-closed operator with the same start and end values represents an empty range. Range operators can express ranges between negative and positive integers, as long as the start value is less than or equal to the end value. Both the start and end values of a range can be retrieved and set, and a range can be checked to see if it is empty:

```
var range1 = 1...5  // Closed range, represents 1, 2, 3, 4, 5
var range2 = 1..<5  // Half-open range, represents 1, 2, 3, 4
let range3 = -3...3 // Closed range, represents -3, -2, -1, 0, 1, 2, 3
range1.startIndex = 5
range1.isEmpty      // False
range2.endIndex = 1
range2.isEmpty      // True
```

> **Note** Closed range operators are represented as their equivalent half-open range operators in output.
>
> ```
> println(1...4) // Prints "1..<5"
> ```

A range operator returns a range, which is implemented as a `struct`:

```
struct Range<T : ForwardIndexType> : Equatable, CollectionType, Printable,
DebugPrintable { ... }
```

This can be read as "A range is a `struct` of some type `T` that conforms to the `ForwardIndexType` protocol, that conforms to the `Equatable`, `CollectionType`, `Printable`, and `DebugPrintable` protocols." This broaches the subjects of protocols and generics, which will be covered in Chapters 8 and 11, respectively, but the purpose of bringing up this detail here is to provide some background before explaining how to represent a range in reverse. As can be deduced from the previous declaration, a range represents value types that conform to the `ForwardIndexType` protocol, which, on further investigation (**command** + **click** on a target such as a protocol to transfer to its definition), means that those values must be integer types (such as `Int` and `UInt`).

> **Tip** In Xcode, to be presented with the option of opening a clicked-on target (such as a function or protocol name) in either the Assistant Editor, an existing or new tab, or an existing or new window, **command** + **option** + **shift** + **click** on the target to open the destination picker. Then either click on your desired destination or use the arrow keys (**command** + arrow keys to switch windows) to navigate around and press **enter** to select a destination (see Figure 5-1).

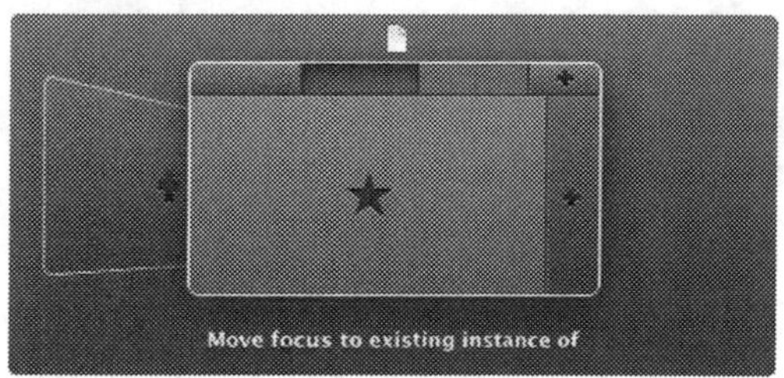

***Figure 5-1.** The destination picker in Xcode*

Because ranges are of forward index integers, the start value must be less than the final value. It is therefore necessary to convert a range to something else in order to represent the range in reverse. First, pass the range to the funtion `lazy()`, which returns a `struct` of type `LazyRandomAccessCollection<Range<Int>>` ("a `LazyRandomAccessCollection` of type `Range` of `Int`"), and then call `reverse()` on that `struct`, which returns a `struct` of type `LazyBidirectionalCollection<RandomAccessReverseView<Range<Int>>>`:

```
let fiveToOne = lazy(1...5).reverse()
for i in fiveToOne {
  print("\(i) ") // Prints "5 4 3 2 1 "
}
```

That being said, and certainly from a more practical standpoint, simply passing a range to `reverse()` will convert the range to an array of the range values in reverse order:

```
let fiveToOne = reverse(1...5) // [5, 4, 3, 2, 1]
```

Tip Taking the time to explore Swift in this manner can be a great way to gain deeper insight into Swift.

`stride()` Functions

Swift includes two functions, `stride(from: to: by:)` and `stride(from: through: by:)`, that return sequence types representing an iteration of values from a start value to/through an end value, by a specified step increment. `stride(from: to: by:)` excludes the final value, and `stride(from: through: by:)` includes the final value. The `from`, `to`/`through`, and `by` values can be integer or floating-point types, however, all three values must be the same type in any one call:

```
let stride1 = stride(from: 10, to: -10, by: -1) // Represents 10, 9, 8,
... to -9 (20 values total)
let stride2 = stride(from: 0.0, through: 3.14, by: 0.1) // Represents 0.0,
0.1, 0.2, ... to 3.14 (32 values total)
```

Control Transfer Statements

Before covering control flow statements, it is necessary to examine the *control transfer statements* that can be used to alter the program flow within a control flow statement, or in one case, a function. Swift offers four such statements—`continue`, `break`, `fallthrough`, and `return`—all of which also exist in Objective-C except `fallthrough`. Of these, only the `fallthrough` statement does not also exist in Objective-C. It is used exclusively with a `switch case` statement, and its usage will be covered in the next section (Conditional Statements). The `return` statement can only be used within a function or method, to include being used within a control flow statement within a function (see the next chapter for additional coverage and examples of usage).

Note In Swift, methods are simply functions that are associated with a type, such as a class. Chapter 6 provides full coverage of functions and methods.

The `continue` and `break` transfer statements work exactly the same in Swift as they do in Objective-C. `continue` is used within a loop to transfer program flow out of the current iteration, to either the beginning of the next iteration of that loop, or, if the loop is in its last iteration, out of the loop altogether, in which case program flow will continue with the next line of code after the loop. break transfers program flow out of a control flow statement immediately. As explained in the Conditional section, switch case statements break by default and thus do not require explicit use of a break statement; however, they must be used for case statements that do not provide at least one executable statement. When used in a loop statement, break will terminate execution of the loop altogether, and transfer program flow to the next line of code after the loop.

Table 5-1 summarizes the behavior of all four control transfer statements, and examples of usage exist throughout the remaining sections of this chapter.

Table 5-1. Control transfer statements in Objective-C and Swift

	Objective-C	Swift
continue	Used within a loop statement to transfer program flow to the beginning of the next iteration of that loop.	Same as Objective-C.
break	Used to transfer program flow to the next line of code after the control flow statement that encloses the break statement.	Same as Objective-C.
fallthrough	N/A; switch case statements automatically fall through to the next case statement, unless a break statement is present.	Used within a switch case statement to transfer to the statement(s) within the next case statement.
return	Transfer program flow out of a method and back to the caller, returning nil implicitly or, optionally, an explicitly specified value (raw or stored) or an expression resulting in a value (either which may be nil) on the same line after return. A specified return value or expression will be casted to the method's return type, or nil if the cast fails.	Same as Objective-C, except the Swift compiler will prevent attempting to specify a return value that cannot be casted to the return type of the function.

Conditional Statements

Conditional statements provide a programmatic fork in the road. Objective-C and Swift both offer two conditional statements: if and switch. However, their implementations and usage differ significantly.

Differences between the if statement in Objective-C and Swift begin with the fact that use of parentheses around the conditional in Swift is optional (and this syntactic noise is discouraged). However, the curly braces are not optional in Swift, even if the body of the if statement is only one line. Additionally, in Objective-C, the conditional statement resolves to a boolean false for a value of 0 or nil, and otherwise, it *resolves* to a boolean true. In Swift, a conditional statement must *equate* to true or false. This can be accomplished by performing an == or != operation, or by using a optional variable or constant, which reports back true if the stored value has a value, or false if it has no value at all (aka nil). Swift also provides a way to create a optional and test it all at once in a conditional, referred to as *optional binding* using the if let (or if var) syntax. Both Objective-C and Swift include the else if and else clauses for use in an if conditional statement.

In Objective-C, a switch statement can only test an integer value (signed or unsigned), which is enclosed in parentheses. In Swift, the parentheses are also optional; yet, more important, *any* type can be tested, such as a Float, a CGPoint, a tuple, or even a custom reference type. Another significant difference is that case statements do not implicitly fall through in Swift. That is, a case statement in Swift must either include a statement, a break statement to explicitly state that the program flow should break out of the switch statement, or a fallthrough keyword to explicitly state that program flow should continue to the statement(s) inside the next case statement. fallthrough is one of four transfer statements in Swift, which will be covered in the Transfer Statements section later in this chapter.

> **Note** The behavior of fallthrough in a Swift switch case is the same as when omitting the break statement for a switch case in Objective-C. Program flow transfers *directly* to the statement inside of the next case statement, without actually evaluating that case statement condition.

A switch statement in Swift must be exhaustive; every possible value must be matched by a case statement or the default catch-all case. Each case in a Swift switch statement can include multiple value matches, and it can also use ranges, value binding, wildcards (_) that will match any value, and even where clauses to check for additional conditions.

Table 5-2 provides comparative examples of if and switch statements in Objective-C and Swift. Recognizing the sheer magnitude of possible use cases of a switch statement in Swift, only a representative sample is provided—further exploration in a playground would be a worthwhile and further eye-opening exercise.

Table 5-2. `if` and `switch` statements in Objective-C and Swift

	Objective-C	Swift
	NSUInteger testScore = 100; typedef enum : NSUInteger { CategoryRecklessDriving, CategoryExhibitionOfAcceleration } Category; NSUInteger speed1 = 50; NSUInteger speed2 = 85; NSUInteger time = 6; Category category;	let testScore = 100 let speedTrap = (speed1: 50, speed2: 85, time: 6)

if	NSString *nameTextFieldText;
	if (nameTextFieldText.length) {
	NSLog(@"Hello %@!", nameTextFieldText);
	} else {
	NSLog(@"Welcome guest!");
	}
	// Prints "Welcome guest!"
		var nameTextFieldText: String?
		if let name = nameTextFieldText {
		println("Hello \(name)!")
		} else {
		println("Welcome guest!")
		}
		// Prints "Welcome guest!"

switch	switch (testScore) {
	case 100:
	printf("You aced it! ");
	case 99:
	case 98:
	printf("Great job! ");
	case YES:
	printf("Your grade: ");
	case 97:
	printf("A+\n");
	break;
	case 96:
	printf("A+\n");
	break;
	case 95:
	printf("A+\n");
	break;
	// Additional cases for 94 down to 80
	(42 lines of code)...
	default:
	printf("Better study more next
	time.\n");
	}
	// Prints "You aced it! Great job!
	Your grade: A+"
		switch testScore {
		case 100:
		print("You aced it! ")
		fallthrough
		case 98, 99:
		print("Great job! ")
		fallthrough
		case 0...100:
		print("Your grade: ")
		fallthrough
		case 95..<100:
		println("A+")
		case 90..<95:
		println("A")
		case 85..<90:
		println("B+")
		case 80..<85:
		println("B")
		default:
		println("Better study more
		next time.")
		}
		// Prints "You aced it! Great
		job! Your grade: A+"

(continued)

Table 5-2. (*continued*)

	Objective-C	Swift

switch	`if (speed2 > 90) {`
	`category = CategoryRecklessDriving;`
	`} else if ((speed2 - speed1) / time`
	`> 4) {`
	`category = CategoryExhibition`
	`OfAcceleration;`
	`}`
	`switch (category) {`
	`case CategoryRecklessDriving:`
	`NSLog(@"Reckless driving");`
	`break;`
	`case CategoryExhibitionOf`
	`Acceleration:`
	`NSLog(@"Exhibition of acceleration");`
	`break;`
	`}`
	`// Prints "Exhibition of`
	`acceleration"`
		`switch speedTrap {`
		`case (_, let s2, _) where`
		`s2 > 90:`
		`println("Reckless driving")`
		`case let (s1, s2, t) where`
		`(s2 - s1) / t > 4:`
		`println("Exhibition of`
		`acceleration")`
		`default:`
		`break`
		`}`
		`// Prints "Exhibition of`
		`acceleration"`

Table 5-3 demonstrates how a common task in Objective-C requiring use of an `if` statement can be performed in Swift using a `switch` instead (Swift function syntax will be covered in Chapter 6).

Table 5-3. Comparing different approaches to a common task in Objective-C and Swift

<table>
<tr><td>Objective-C</td><td><pre>- (void)prepareForSegue:(UIStoryboardSegue *)segue
sender:(id)sender
{
  if ([segue.identifier isEqualToString:@"Item Detail"]) {
     DetailViewController *d = (DetailViewController *)
     segue.destinationViewController;
     d.title = segue.identifier;
     d.itemForDetail = item;
  } else if ([segue.identifier isEqualToString:@"Related
  Items"]) {
   UINavigationController *nc = segue.destinationViewController;
   RelatedViewController *r = (RelatedViewController *)
   nc.topViewController;
   r.title = segue.identifier;
   r.category = item.category;
  }</pre></td></tr>
<tr><td>Swift</td><td><pre>override func prepareForSegue(segue: UIStoryboardSegue!,
sender: AnyObject!) {
  switch (segue.identifier, segue.destinationViewController) {
  case let (i, d as DetailViewController) where i == "Item
  Detail":
    d.title = i
    d.itemForDetail = item
  case let (i, nc as UINavigationController) where
  i == "Related Items":
    let r = nc.topViewController as RelatedViewController
    r.title = i
    r.category = item.category
   default:
   break;
  }
}</pre></td></tr>
</table>

The while and do-while statements combine conditional checking with the ability to repeatedly (and possibly indefinitely) loop over a set of statements. They work similarly in Objective-C and Swift, except that the parentheses enclosing the conditional statement are optional in Swift (see Table 5-4).

Table 5-4. `while` *and* `do-while` *statements in Objective-C and Swift*

	Objective-C	Swift

	`- (u_int32_t)rollDie`
	`{`
	`  return arc4random_uniform(6) + 1;`
	`}`
	`int die1 = [self rollDie];`
	`int die2 = [self rollDie];`
		`func rollDie () -> UInt32 {`
		`  return arc4random_uniform(6) + 1`
		`}`
		`var die1 = rollDie()`
		`var die2 = rollDie()`

while	`while (die1 != 1 && die2 != 1) {`
	`  NSLog(@"%u & %u", die1, die2);`
	`  die1 = [self rollDie];`
	`  die2 = [self rollDie];`
	`}`
	`NSLog(@"Snake eyes!");`
		`while die1 != 1 && die2 != 1 {`
		`println("\(die1) & \(die2)")`
		`  die1 = rollDie()`
		`  die2 = rollDie()`
		`}`
		`println("Snake eyes!")`

do-while	`do {`
	`  die1 = [self rollDie];`
	`  die2 = [self rollDie];`
	`  NSLog(@"%u & %u", die1, die2);`
	`} while (die1 != 1 && die2 != 1);`
	`  NSLog(@"Snake eyes!");`
		`do {`
		`  die1 = rollDie()`
		`  die2 = rollDie()`
		`println("\(die1) & \(die2)")`
		`} while die1 != 1 && die2 != 1`
		`println("Snake eyes!")`

Iteration and Enumeration

Control flow looping statements enable iterating through a numerical range of indexes or enumerating over a collection of values. Swift's range operators and `stride()` functions provide for quick and easy iteration of numerical indexes, and should be the go-to choice for such needs. For example, these two for loops do the same thing:

```
for var i = 0; i < 5; i++ {
  // ...
}
for i in 0..<5 {
  // ...
}
```

Objective-C includes the basic `for` loop iteration statement, a `for-in` loop statement for "fast enumeration" of objects that conform to the `NSFastEnumeration` protocol, and object and block-based enumerators for the collection classes.

Swift's for (aka "for-condition-increment") and for-in loop statements look and behave just like their Objective-C counterparts (except the parentheses are once again optional). When used with an array, for-in will return each sequential member of the array. When used with a dictionary, for-in will decompose each key-value pair into a tuple of (key, value).

Similar to using for-in with Objective-C's -[NSDictionary allKeys] and -[NSDictionary allValues] methods, for-in in Swift can be used with a dictionary's keys or values properties. Keep in mind that the sort order is undefined—although, while that truly means the order will seem random in Objective-C, in Swift, both the keys and values properties appear to return the list sorted ascending by the key.

Swift also includes a global enumerate() function. Its primary use is with arrays in a for-in statement, returning a tuple of (index, value) for each array element. However, enumerate() can also be used with a dictionary, returning a tuple of (tupleIndex, (key, value)) for each entry, should the need arise to enumerate a dictionary in this manner. enumerate() can also be used with a String, in which case it will decompose the string into tuples of (tupleIndex, character). Table 5-5 includes a variety of iteration and enumeration examples in Objective-C and Swift.

Table 5-5. *Iteration and enumeration statements in Objective-C and Swift*

	Objective-C	Swift
	`NSDictionary *numbers = @{@1: @"One", @2: @"Two", @3: @"Three"};` `NSString *starring = @"STARRING";`	`let numbers = [1: "One", 2: "Two", 3: "Three"]`

for	`for (int i = 1; i < 4; i++) {`
	`   printf("%i ", i);`
	`}`
	`// Prints "1 2 3 "`
		`for i in 1...3 {`
		`   print("\(i) ")`
		`}`
		`// Prints "1 2 3 "`

for	`for (int i = 10; i > 0; i -= 2) {`
	`   printf("%i ", i);`
	`}`
	`// Prints "10 8 6 4 2 "`
		`for i in stride(from: 10, to: 0, by: -2) {`
		`   print("\(i) ")`
		`}`
		`// Prints "10 8 6 4 2 "`

(continued)

Table 5-5. (*continued*)

	Objective-C	Swift

for-in	`for (NSNumber *n in [numbers allKeys]) {`
	`  if ([n isEqual:@2]) {`
	`  continue;`
	`  }`
	`NSLog(@"%@: %@", n, numbers[n]);`
	`}`
	`// Prints "3: Three`
	`1: One"`
		`for (k, v) in numbers {`
		`  if k == 2 {`
		`  continue`
		`  }`
		`println("\(k): \(v)")`
		`}`
		`// Prints "1: One`
		`3: Three"`

for-in	`for (NSNumber *i in [[@[@1, @2, @3] reverseObjectEnumerator] allObjects]) {`
	`  printf("%i ", [i integerValue]);`
	`}`
	`// Prints "3 2 1 "`
		`for i in reverse(1...3) {`
		`  print("\(i) ")`
		`}`
		`// Prints "3 2 1 "`

for-in	`NSRange range = NSMakeRange(0, 1);`
	`for (; range.location < starring.length; range.location++) {`
	`  NSLog(@"%@", [starring substringWithRange:range]);`
	`}`
	`// Prints each letter of "STARRING" on a new line`
		`for c in enumerate("STARRING") {`
		`  println(c.1)`
		`}`
		`// Prints each letter of "STARRING" on a new line`

Labels

In order to provide explicit control over program flow within `switch` statements that are nested within other `switch` statements or looping statements, `switch` and looping statements in Swift can optionally be labeled and then subsequently referred to by their label in control transfer statements.

This capability most closely resemble's Objective-C's `goto` statement, which can be used in conjunction with a `label:` identifier to jump from a `goto` to a `label:` so long as it is within the same method or function. Table 5-6 compares these features between Objective-C and Swift, albeit using highly contrived examples.

Table 5-6. Comparing labels in Objective-C and Swift

<table>
<tr><td>Objective-C</td><td><pre>start:
while (true) {
    int randomNumber = arc4random_uniform(100);
    switch (randomNumber) {
      case 55:
        printf(" - Finally!\n");
        goto end;
      default:
      printf("\nrandomNumber = %i", randomNumber);
      goto start;
    }
}
end:
printf("\n");</pre></td></tr>
<tr><td>Swift</td><td><pre>start: while true {
    let randomNumber = arc4random_uniform(100)
    switch randomNumber {
      case 55:
        println(" - Finally!")
        break start
      case 0...100:
        println()
        print("randomNumber = \(randomNumber)")
        continue start
        default:
        break
    }
}</pre></td></tr>
</table>

Summary

This chapter examined how to control program flow in Swift using mechanisms that are similar to that provided by Objective-C, as well as taking advantage of entirely new capabilities provided by Swift. Of these control flow constructs, the `switch` statement is greatly improved on in Swift to make it the preferred choice for conditional statements of more than a couple possible branches, and the new range operator and `stride()` functions offer significantly streamlined approaches to iteration.

Chapter 6

Creating Functions

Swift functions are actually a type of closure, and Swift's implementation of closures is both flexible and powerful—ranging from anonymous inline closures similar to Objective-C blocks, to complex functions extending far beyond the capabilities of an Objective-C method.

Swift functions are named closures that operate similarly to Objective-C methods. Closures can also be unnamed (aka, anonymous), in which case they are referred to as *closure expressions*. Closure expressions resemble Objective-C blocks that were introduced with iOS 4 and Mac OS X 10.6 in 2010—reportedly and coincidentally right around the time development of Swift began.

This chapter will compare Objective-C methods and blocks to Swift's functions and closure expressions, respectively. Since function syntax is also used to overload existing operators and create new custom operators, both tasks will also be covered in this chapter.

Methods & Functions

Objective-C methods:

- Are specific to classes
- Must be uniquely named and cannot be overloaded
- Are intended to be either public or private
- Have an optional yet defined set of parameters
- May optionally return a single value

Swift functions:

- Are global or specific to a type (with varying levels of access)
- Can be overloaded
- Can have multiple and/or variadic parameters
- Can be nested within other functions or passed as parameters to other functions
- Can optionally return a single value or multiple values including functions
- Can be assigned to a variable or constant (remember from Chapter 2 that closures are reference types, passed by reference vs. copy)

Additionally, classes, structures, and enumerations in Swift can all define functions (see the next chapter for details).

> **Tip** Swift functions that are defined within a type are referred to as *methods*. However, the terms *function* and *method* are used interchangibly in Apple's documentation referring to functions of a particular type.

The syntax of Objective-C methods and Swift functions is similar. Most notably, Swift uses a `func` keyword, encloses the parameters in parentheses, and moves the return type to the end proceeding an `->`. Table 6-1 compares the basic syntax of an Objective-C method and Swift function.

***Table 6-1.** Basic syntax of an Objective-C method and Swift function*

Objective-C	`- (ReturnType)methodNameParamOne:(ParamType) paramOneName paramTwo:(ParamType)paramTwoName {`
	`    statements`
	`}`

Swift	`func functionName(paramOneName: ParamType, paramTwoName: ParamType) -> ReturnType {`
	`    statements`
	`}`

Table 6-1 compared the syntax of Objective-C instance method to what could be a global Swift function, or an instance method defined within a class, structure, or enumeration type. The next chapter will delve into creating these types and their associated methods. It is enough to mention now, however, that these types can also define *type methods*, equivalent to class methods in Objective-C. The only difference in syntax for defining a type method is to begin the definition with the keyword `static` in the case of structures and enumerations, or `class` in the case of classes, comparable to using the + method type identifier in Objective-C to signify a class method. Table 6-2 compares the basic syntax to define a class method in Objective-C and type method in Swift, this time also demonstrating that a Swift function that takes no parameters and returns no value simply includes an empty set of parentheses for the input and omits the return syntax altogether.

Table 6-2. *Basic syntax of an Objective-C class method and Swift type method*

Objective-C	`+ (void)methodName`
	`{`
	`    statements`
	`}`

Swift	`static func functionName() {`
	`    statements`
	`}`

The similarities and differences between Objective-C methods and Swift functions will be examined next, including introduction of new capabilities provided in Swift. Tables 6-3 and 6-4 will then list several comparable examples. For simplicity's sake, the Objective-C methods are presumed to be implemented in the same class and called in another method within that same class, such as custom instance methods defined in a `UIViewController` instance and called in `-[UIViewController viewDidLoad]`.

As in Objective-C methods, parameters in Swift fuctions are only available within the scope of the function, thus called *local parameter names*. Local parameter names are not used when calling a function; only the argument value(s) are passed. To improve readability, Swift functions can also define *external parameter names* for use when calling the function, resulting in a function signature that closely resembles the inline parameter name syntax of Objective-C methods. If defined, external parameter names must be used when calling the function. An external name can be the same as or different than the local parameter name with which it is paired.

> **Tip** Prefixing a local parameter name with a hash symbol (#) in a function definition is a shorthand syntax way to define an external parameter name that is the same as the local parameter name.

> **Note** Swift methods (i.e., functions defined within a type) automatically create external parameter names for the second and subsequent parameters, unless explicitly defined. This will be covered in full in the next chapter.

Unlike Objective-C, in which parameters are by default passed by copy and mutable within the scope of the function, Swift function parameters are constants by default, thus immutable within the function. However, similar to mutability of items added to collections, the items in a collection, or properties of a reference type, when passed as a parameter in a function, are mutable to the extent of those individual items or properties—even though the parameter value itself is not mutable (i.e., cannot be reassigned). Although parameters are by default constants in a Swift function, it is possible to have the function create a mutable copy of the parameter, by explicity declaring the parameter as a variable using the `var` prefix. Known as *variable parameters*, these parameters are mutable (i.e., can be reassigned) within the scope of the function. It is also possible to allow a function to modify the original variable being passed in as a parameter, such that those changes persist after the function has ended. To enable this behavior, prefix the parameter with the keyword `inout` in the function definition, and prefix the parameter name with an ampersand (&) when calling the function. Using `inout` parameters in Swift is akin to passing by reference in Objective-C, i.e., defining the parameter as a pointer reference (** for objects and * for scalars), prefixing the parameter with an & when calling the function, and dereferencing the value within the body of the method by prefixing it with an *. These mutability rules are logical, although they may be a little overwhelming at first. Examples in Table 6-3 and the summary of parameter mutability rules in Table 6-5 should help to form a solid understanding.

Objective-C does not allow setting default values for parameters. One workaround is pass and check for `nil` (or `[NSNull null]` et al., accordingly). Swift offers built-in support for setting default parameter values, which should be placed after parameters without default values to ensure proper order when calling the method. Unless explicitly defined, external parameter names are automatically created for parameters with default values. Although not advisable under most circumstances, it is possible to opt out of this behavior by writing an underscore (_) for the external name of a parameter.

Objective-C enables defining a method that can take a variadic parameter, requiring a `nil`-terminated list to be passed for the variadic parameter, and processing the list using a handful of C functions. Swift streamlines this process significantly. Both Objective-C and Swift utilize an ellipsis (`...`) to define a variadic parameter. And just like an Objective-C method, a Swift function can have only one variadic parameter, which also must be placed last in the parameter list.

Swift functions can return a value, just like an Objective-C method. A Swift function can also return multiple values, using a tuple. Keeping Swift's optionals in mind—that is, that an optional value can either have a value or be `nil`—Swift functions can return an optional value, an optional tuple, or a tuple containing one or more optionals. Remember from Chapter 2 that optional values must be unwrapped before use, such as by using optional binding or force unwrapping.

In Objective-C, a scalar value being passed as a parameter or returned as a value of a different scalar type will be implicitly converted to the parameter or return type. However, the conversion may not be successful or may produce unexpected results. In Swift, a parameter or return value type value must be of the type specified. Therefore, a value type of differing type will need to be converted to the parameter or return type beforehand, either using an initializer of the specified parameter or return type, if available, or else manual conversion will be necessary (if not a different design of the function made altogether).

When dealing with class types in either Objective-C or Swift, a subclass may be passed or returned as a parent class type. The opposite of course is not true, that is, a value of a parent class cannot be passed or returned for an expected sublass type of that parent class. However, if the value is believed to actually be an instance of the required subclass type for the parameter or return value, it must be explicitly casted as that subclass type beforehand in Swift, using the `as` or `as?` operator (the latter requiring appropriate `nil` checking and/or changing the type to an optional of the specified type). In Objective-C, in addition to casting the value as the expected parameter or return type, defensive checks such as `-[NSObject isKindOfClass:]` or `-[NSObject respondsToSelector:]` are also necessary. Subclassing will be covered in Chapter 9, and methods (functions of a type), as used in the Swift Single return value (subclass) example in Table 6-4, will be further described in the next chapter.

A Swift function's *function type* is made up of its input parameter type(s) and return type, for example, the function type `(Int, String) -> Bool` defines a function that takes an `Int` and `String` and returns a `Bool`:

```
func integer(integer: Int, equalsString string: String) -> Bool {
  return integer == string.toInt()
}
integer(1, equalsString: "2") // False
```

A function that takes no inputs and returns no value has a function type of `() -> ()`. Function types are also used to define function parameter types and return types, essentially working like a prototype to define a blueprint that the function parameter must implement (see coverage of prototypes in Chapter 8):

```
// A function that takes a function as a parameter
func processString(string: String, withSomeFunction someFunction: (String)
-> ()) {
  someFunction(string)
}
func printString(string: String) {
  println(string)
}
processString("Hello world", withSomeFunction: printString)
// Prints "Hello world"

// A function that returns a function
func printer() -> (String) -> () {
  func somePrintingFunction(string: String) {
    println(string)
  }
  return somePrintingFunction
}
let printFunction = printer()
printFunction("Hello world") // Prints "Hello world"
```

Table 6-3. *Comparing parameter input scenarios in Objective-C methods and Swift functions*

	Objective-C	Swift

No parameters	`- (void)printTime`
	`{`
	`  NSString *timestamp = [NSDateFormatter localizedStringFromDate:[NSDate date] dateStyle:NSDateFormatterMediumStyle timeStyle:NSDateFormatterShortStyle];`
	`    NSLog(@"%@", timestamp);`
	`}`
	`[self printTime]; // Prints current timestamp, e.g., "Sep 9, 2014, 4:30 AM"`
		`func printTime() {`
		`  let timestamp = NSDateFormatter.localizedStringFromDate(NSDate(), dateStyle: .MediumStyle, timeStyle: .ShortStyle)`
		`    println(timestamp)`
		`}`
		`printTime() // Prints current timestamp, e.g., "Sep 9, 2014, 4:30 AM"`

Single parameter	`- (void)printUnicodeNameForCharacter:(NSString *)character`
	`{`
	`  CFMutableStringRef cfMutableString = (__bridge CFMutableStringRef)([NSMutableString stringWithFormat:@"%@", character]);`
	`  CFRange range = CFRangeMake(0, CFStringGetLength(cfMutableString));`
	`  CFStringTransform(cfMutableString, &range, kCFStringTransformToUnicodeName, 0);`
	`  NSString *cString = [NSString stringWithFormat:@"%@", cfMutableString];`
	`  NSString *unicodeName = [cString substringWithRange:NSMakeRange(3, cString.length - 4)];`
	`  NSLog(@"%@", unicodeName.capitalizedString);`
	`}`
	`[self printUnicodeNameForCharacter:@"•"]; // Prints "Caduceus"`
		`func printUnicodeName(#character: Character) {`
		`  let cfMutabeString = NSMutableString(string: String(character)) as CFMutableString`
		`  var range = CFRangeMake(0, CFStringGetLength(cfMutabeString))`
		`CFStringTransform(cfMutabeString, &range, kCFStringTransformToUnicodeName, 0)`
		`  let cString = "\(cfMutabeString)"`
		`  let startIndex = advance(cString.startIndex, 3)`
		`  let endIndex = advance(cString.endIndex, -1)`
		`  let unicodeName = cString.substringWithRange(Range(startIndex..<endIndex))`
		`println(unicodeName.capitalizedString)`
		`}`
		`printUnicodeName(character: "⚕")`
		`// Prints "Caduceus"`

(continued)

Table 6-3. (*continued*)

<table>
<tr><th></th><th>Objective-C</th><th>Swift</th></tr>
<tr><td>Single parameter (subclass)</td><td><pre>@interface MyClass : NSObject
@end
@implementation MyClass
@end
@interface MySubClass : MyClass
@end
@implementation MySubClass
@end
- (void)doSomethingWithMyClass:(MyClass *)myClass
{
  // ...
}
[self doSomethingWithMyClass:[MySubClass new]];</pre></td><td><pre>class MyClass { }
class MySubClass: MyClass { }
func doSomethingWithMyClass(myClass: MyClass) {
  // ...
}
doSomethingWithMyClass(MySubClass())</pre></td></tr>
<tr><td>Default parameter</td><td><pre>- (void)concatenateArrayOfStrings:(NSArray *)strings
withSeparator:(NSString *)separator
{
  separator = separator ?: @", ";
  __block NSMutableString *string = [@"" mutableCopy];
  [strings enumerateObjectsUsingBlock:^(NSString *s,
  NSUInteger idx, BOOL *stop) {
    if (idx == 0) {
      [string appendFormat:@"%@", s];
    } else if (idx < [strings count] - 1) {
      [string appendFormat:@"%@%@", separator, s];
    } else {</pre></td><td><pre>func concatenateArrayOfStrings
(strings: [String], withSeparator separator: String
= ", ") {
  var string = ""
  for (i, s) in enumerate(strings) {
    switch i {
    case 0:
      string = strings[0]
    case 1..<strings.endIndex - 1:
      string += (separator + s)</pre></td></tr>
</table>

	[string appendFormat:@", and %@", s];
	    }
	  }];
	  NSLog(@"%@", string);
	}
	
	[self concatenateArrayOfStrings:@[@"Scott", @"Lori", @"Charlotte", @"Betty", @"Gracie", @"Sophie", @"Stella", @"Isabella", @"Lilith", @"Darby"] withSeparator:nil]; // Prints "Scott, Lori, Charlotte, Betty, Gracie, Sophie, Stella, Isabella, Lilith, and Darby"
		default:
		      string += (", and \(s).")
		    }
		  }
		  println(string)
		}
		concatenateArrayOfStrings(["Scott", "Lori", "Charlotte", "Betty", "Gracie", "Sophie", "Stella", "Isabella", "Lilith", "Darby"]) // Prints "Scott, Lori, Charlotte, Betty, Gracie, Sophie, Stella, Isabella, Lilith, and Darby."

Multiple parameters	@import AVFoundation;
	- (void)sayGreeting:(NSString *)greeting toName:(NSString *)name
	{
	  AVSpeechUtterance *utterance = [AVSpeechUtterance speechUtteranceWithString:[NSString stringWithFormat:@"%@ %@", greeting ?: @"Hello", name ?: @"world"]];
	  AVSpeechSynthesizer *synthesizer = [AVSpeechSynthesizer new];
	  [synthesizer speakUtterance:utterance];
	}
	[self sayGreeting:@"Hi" toName:@"Scott"]; // Speaks "Hi Scott" (works on device only)
		import AVFoundation
		func sayGreeting(greeting: String?, toName name: String?) {
		  let theGreeting = greeting ?? "Hello"
		  let theName = name ?? "World"
		  let utterance = AVSpeechUtterance(string: "\(theGreeting) \(theName)")
		  let synthesizer = AVSpeechSynthesizer()
		  synthesizer.speakUtterance(utterance)
		}
		sayGreeting("Hi", toName: "Scott") // Speaks "Hi Scott" (works on device only)

(continued)

Table 6-3. (*continued*)

	Objective-C	Swift

Variadic parameter	- (void)printHtmlTR:(NSString *)tdValue, ...
	{
	NSMutableString *tr = [@"<tr>" mutableCopy];
	va_list tdValues;
	va_start(tdValues, tdValue);
	for (; tdValue; tdValue = va_arg(tdValues, NSString *))
	{
	[tr appendFormat:@"<td>%@</td>", tdValue];
	}
	va_end(tdValues);
	[tr appendString:@"</tr>"];
	NSLog(@"%@", tr);
	}
	[self printHtmlTR:@"5 bananas", @"@ $1 each", @"= $5", nil]; // Print "<tr><td>5 bananas </td><td>@ $1 each</td><td>= $5</td></tr>"
		func printHtmlTR(tdValues: String...) {
		var tr = "<tr>"
		for tdValue in tdValues {
		tr += ("<td>" + tdValue + "</td>")
		}
		tr += "</tr>"
		println(tr)
		}
		printHtmlTR("5 bananas", "@ $1 each", "= $5")
		// Print "<tr><td>5 bananas</td><td>@ $1 each</td><td>= $5</td>
		</tr>"

Pass by reference parameter	- (int)square:(int)integer
	{
	return integer * integer;
	}
	int squareOf5 = [self square:5]; // Prints "25"
		func square(inout integer: Int) {
		integer *= integer
		}
		var number = 5
		square(&number)
		println(number) // Prints "25"

Table 6-4. Comparing return value scenarios in Objective-C methods and Swift functions

	Objective-C	Swift

No return value	`- (void)printOutGreeting:(NSString *)greeting toPerson:(NSString *)person`
	`{`
	`  NSLog(@"%@ %@!", greeting, person);`
	`}`
	`[self printOutGreeting:@"Hello" toPerson:@"Scott"];`
	`// Prints "Hello Scott!"`
		`func printOut(#greeting: String, toPerson person: String) {`
		`  println("\(greeting) \(person)!")`
		`}`
		`printOut(greeting: "Hello", toPerson: "Scott")`
		`// Prints "Hello Scott!"`

Single return value	`- (NSInteger)addInteger:(NSInteger)n1 toInteger:(NSInteger)n2`
	`{`
	`  return n1 + n2;`
	`}`
	`NSInteger onePlusTwo = [self addInteger:1 toInteger:2];`
	`// 3`
		`func addInteger(n1: Int, toInteger n2: Int) -> Int {`
		`  return n1 + n2`
		`}`
		`let onePlusTwo = addInteger(1, toInteger: 2)`
		`// 3`

(continued)

Table 6-4. (*continued*)

	Objective-C	Swift

Single return value (subclass)	@interface MyClass : NSObject
	@end
	@implementation MyClass
	@end
	@interface MySubClass : MyClass
	- (void)printMySubClass;
	@end
	@implementation MySubClass
	- (void)printMySubClass
	{
	  NSLog(@"MySubClass");
	}
	@end
	- (MySubClass *)returnMySubClass:(MyClass *)myClass
	{
	  return (MySubClass *)myClass;
	}
	NSArray *someClasses = @[[MySubClass new], [MyClass new]];
	[someClasses enumerateObjectsUsingBlock:^(id item, NSUInteger idx, BOOL *stop) {
	  MySubClass *mySubClass = [self returnMySubClass:item];
	  if ([mySubClass isKindOfClass:[MySubClass class]]) {
	    [item printMySubClass];
	  }
	}];
	// Prints "MySubClass" for the first item only, since the second item is not a MySubClass type
		class MyClass { }
		class MySubClass: MyClass {
		  func printMySubClass() {
		    println("MySubClass")
		  }
		}
		func returnMySubClass(myClass: MyClass) -> MySubClass? {
		  return myClass as? MySubClass
		}
		let someClasses: [MyClass] = [MySubClass(), MyClass()]
		for (idx, item) in enumerate(someClasses) {
		  if let mySubClass = returnMySubClass(item) {
		    mySubClass.printMySubClass()// Prints "MySubClass" for the first item only, since the second item was not successfully downcasted
		  }
		}

Single return value (converted)

```
- (CGFloat)convertToFloat:(NSInteger)integer
{
  return integer;
}
NSLog(@"%f", [self convertToFloat:1]);
// Prints "1.000000"
```

```
func convertToFloat(integer: Int) -> Float {
  return Float(integer)
}
println(convertToFloat(1)) // Prints "1.0"
```

Single optional return value

```
- (NSString *)addString:(NSString *)string1
toString:(NSString *)string2
{
  NSString *total;
  NSInteger n1 = [string1 integerValue];
  NSInteger n2 = [string2 integerValue];
  if ((n1 || [string1 isEqualToString:@"0"]) && (n2 ||
  [string2 isEqualToString:@"0"])) {
    total = [NSString stringWithFormat:@"%li", (long)n1
    + (long)n2];
  }
  return total;
}
NSString *addTwoIntegerStrings = [self addString:@"0"
toString:@"-1"];
if (addTwoIntegerStrings) {
  NSLog(@"%@",  addTwoIntegerStrings);
}
// Prints "-1"
```

```
func addString(string1: String, toString string2:
String) -> String? {
  var total: String?
  if let n1 = string1.toInt() {
    if let n2 = string2.toInt() {
      total = String(n1 + n2)
    }
  }
  return total
}
if let result = addString("1", toString: "2") {
  println(result)
}
// Prints "3"
```

(continued)

Table 6-4. (*continued*)

	Objective-C	Swift

Multiple return values	- (NSArray *)getIntegerAndNumberSpelledOutForNumberString:
	(NSString *)numberString
	{
	NSNumber *number = @([numberString integerValue]);
	NSNumberFormatter *spellOutFormatter =
	[NSNumberFormatter new];
	spellOutFormatter.numberStyle = NSNumberFormatter
	SpellOutStyle;
	return @[number, [spellOutFormatter
	stringFromNumber:number]];
	}
	NSArray *numberStringAsIntegerAndSpelledOut =
	[self getIntegerAndNumberSpelled
	OutForNumberString:@"101"];
	NSLog(@"%@", numberStringAsIntegerAndSpelledOut);
	// Prints '(101, "one hundred one")'
		func getIntegerAndNumberSpelledOutForNumberString
		(numberString: String) -> (Int, String)! {
		var returnTuple: (Int, String)?
		let spellOutFormatter = NSNumberFormatter()
		spellOutFormatter.numberStyle = .SpellOutStyle
		if let number = numberString.toInt() {
		let nsNumber = NSNumber(integer: number)
		returnTuple = (number, spellOutFormatter.
		stringFromNumber(number))
		}
		return returnTuple
		}
		println(getIntegerAndNumberSpelledOutForNumberString
		("101")) // Prints "(101, one hundred one)"

As previously mentioned, Swift functions can take functions as parameters, nest other functions, and return functions. The following example does all three. `formatNumberAsSpelledOutString()` is a helper function that, along with two numbers (of type `Int` or `Double`) is passed to `printOutSumOfNumber(_:andNumber:withFormatter:)`, and it returns a `printResult()` function that can be called inline (as in the example, by appending () to the end of the function call), or stored and called later:

```
func formatNumberAsSpelledOutString(number: Any) -> String {
  var numberString: String!
  let spellOutFormatter = NSNumberFormatter()
  spellOutFormatter.numberStyle = .SpellOutStyle
  if number is Int {
    let num = number as Int
    numberString = spellOutFormatter.stringFromNumber(num)
  } else if number is Double {
    spellOutFormatter.minimumFractionDigits = 1
    let num = number as Double
    numberString = spellOutFormatter.stringFromNumber(num)
  } else {
    numberString = "NaN"
  }
  return numberString
}

func printOutSumOfNumber(var number1: Any, var andNumber number2: Any,
withFormatter formatter: (Any) -> String) -> () -> () {
  var result: String!
  func addTwoIntegers(int1: Any, int2: Any) -> Int {
    let num1 = int1 as Int
    let num2 = int2 as Int
    let sum = num1 + num2
    return sum
  }
  func addTwoDoubles(int1: Any, int2: Any) -> Double {
    let num1 = int1 as Double
    let num2 = int2 as Double
    let sum = num1 + num2
    return sum
  }
  func printResult() {
    println("The sum of \(formatter(number1)) and \(formatter(number2)) is
\(result).")
  }
```

```
  switch (number1, number2) {
  case (is Int, is Int):
    number1 = number1 as Int
    number2 = number2 as Int
    let sum = addTwoIntegers(number1, number2)
    result = formatter(sum)
  case (is Int, is Double):
    number1 = Double(number1 as Int)
    number2 = number2 as Double
    let sum = addTwoDoubles(number1, number2)
    result = formatter(sum)
  case (is Double, is Int):
    number1 = number1 as Double
    number2 = Double(number2 as Int)
    let sum = addTwoDoubles(number1, number2)
    result = formatter(sum)
  case (is Double, is Double):
    number1 = number1 as Double
    number2 = number2 as Double
    let sum = addTwoDoubles(number1, number2)
    result = formatter(sum)
  default:
    result = formatter("")
  }
  return printResult
}
printOutSumOfNumber(1, andNumber: 0.23, withFormatter:
formatNumberAsSpelledOutString)() // Prints "The sum of one and zero point
two three is one point two three."
```

Objective-C can achieve similar results using blocks, as can closure expressions in Swift. This will be covered in the section Blocks and Closure Expressions.

Table 6-5. Summary of parameter mutability in Objective-C methods and Swift functions

	Collection	Object/Reference Type
Objective-C		
Mutable (copy)	Original object must be mutable Can be reassigned Values can be reassigned Values can be added or removed Mutable values are modifiable Changes do not persist outside of method	Can be reassigned Mutable properties are modifiable Changes do not persist outside of method
Immutable (copy)	Cannot be reassigned Values cannot be added or removed Values cannot be reassigned Mutable values are modifiable Changes do not persist outside of method	Can be reassigned Mutable properties are modifiable Changes do not persist outside of method
Passed by reference	Can be reassigned Values can be added or removed if original collection is mutable Mutable values are modifiable Changes persist outside of method	Can be reassigned Mutable properties are modifiable Changes persist outside of method
Swift		
Default (constant)	Cannot be reassigned Values cannot be added or removed Variable values are modifiable Changes persist outside of function	Cannot be reassigned Variable properties are modifiable Changes persist outside of function

(*continued*)

Table 6-5. (*continued*)

	Collection	Object/Reference Type
Variable (copy)	Can be reassigned Values can be added or removed from arrays or dictionaries (not tuples) Variable values are modifiable Changes do not persist outside of function	Can be reassigned Variable values are modifiable Variable properties are modifiable Changes do not persist outside of function
inout (variable)	Original value must be a variable (not constant) Can be reassigned Values can be added or removed from arrays or dictionaries (not tuples) Variable values are modifiable Changes persist outside of function	Original value must be a variable (not constant) Can be reassigned Variable properties are modifiable Changes persist outside of function

Currying

Currying is a functional programming technique that can be used to replace a multiparameter function with a single-parameter *curried function*, such that the curried function can remember one or more bound parameter values (i.e., arguments) that can be used in sequential calls of the curried function. Objective-C does not provide true support for currying, although clever implementations that achieve a similar effect can be found online. Swift supports currying outright, and offers a specific syntax for defining a curried function:

```
func functionName(parameter1)(parameter2) -> (ReturnType) {
  statements
}
```

This can be read as "functionName takes parameter1 and returns a function that takes parameter2 and returns a ReturnType." In this example, parameter1 is bound when initially calling the function, which returns a function that can be subsequently called and passed a single parameter (parameter2), and it returns a ReturnType. As mentioned, one or more arguments can be initially bound and used in forthcoming calls to the single-parameter curried function:

```
import Foundation
func addLineItem(product: String, #price: Double)(quantity: Int) -> (String)
{
  var discountMultiplier: Double
  switch quantity {
  case 1...10:
    discountMultiplier = 1.0
  case 11...20:
    discountMultiplier = 0.9
  default:
    discountMultiplier = 0.8
  }
  return String(format: "\(quantity) of \(product) at $%.2f each = $%.2f",
  price * discountMultiplier, price * Double(quantity) * discountMultiplier)
}
let sellPinotNoir = addLineItem("Pinot Noir", price: 125.0)
var lineItem = sellPinotNoir(quantity: 5)
println(lineItem) // Prints "5 of Pinot Noir at $125.00 each = $625.00"
lineItem = sellPinotNoir(quantity: 25)
println(lineItem) // Prints "25 of Pinot Noir at $100.00 each = $2500.00"
```

Overloading

Objective-C methods must have a unique method name, which is to say that Objective-C methods cannot be overloaded by changing the parameters and/or return type. Swift functions can be overloaded. The overall signature, including the parameters and return type, is evaluated for uniqueness by the compiler. The following example illustrates multiple overloads of the same method name with differing parameter and return values, and Figure 6-1 shows the code-completion popup that appears when beginning to type the function "processI..." within the same scope:

```
func processInput(input: String) {
  // ...
}

func processInput(input: String) -> Bool {
  // ...
  return true
}
```

```
func processInput(input: String) -> Int {
  // ...
  return 1
}

func processInput(input: Int) -> Bool {
  // ...
  return true
}

func processInput(input: Int) {
  // ...
}
```

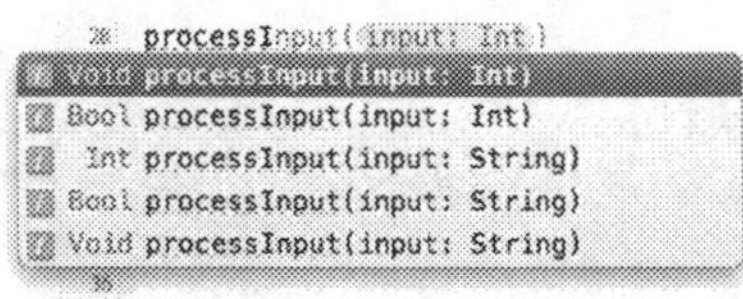

***Figure 6-1.** Code-completion for overloaded function in Swift*

Overloading is not limited to functions. As mentioned in Chapter 4, operators can also be overloaded, and, in fact, the pattern matching operator (~=) is intended for that purpose; by default, ~= is equivalent to ==:

```
func ~= (string: String, integer: Int) -> Bool {
  return string == "\(integer)"
}

func ~= (integer: Int, string: String) -> Bool {
  return "\(integer)" == string
}
println("1" ~= 1) // Prints "true"
println(1 ~= "1") // Prints "true"
```

> **Note** The assignment (=) and ternary conditional (`?:`, as in `a ? b : c`) operators cannot be overloaded.

Custom Operators

Swift facilitates creating entirely new operators, with only a few limitations. Custom operators can begin with any one of the ASCII characters /, =, -, +, !, *, %, <, >, &, |, ^, ?, ~, or one of the Unicode math, symbol, arrow, dingbat, or line/box drawing characters. The second and subsequent characters of a custom operator can be of any of the previously mentioned characters, and/or a Unicode combining character. A custom operator can also be defined as a series of two or more dots (such as ....). Consult Apple's Swift language guide for a complete list of Unicode characters permissible for use in custom operators (`http://bit.ly/swiftlexicalstructure`).

> **Note** The tokens `->`, `//`, `/*`, `*/`, `.`, and the prefix & (used to indicate pass-by-reference for an `inout` parameter) cannot be used alone as custom operators but can be used in combination with additional permissible characters.

Custom operators must first be declared at a global level using the operator keyword, preceded by the `prefix`, `infix`, or `postfix` modifier to indicate the operator *fixity*. Precedence and associativity may optionally be specified for custom `infix` operators, defaulting to `100` and `none` if not specified, respectively (consult Table 4-8 in Chapter 4 for a listing of precedence and associativity classifications for Swift's built-in binary operators). Subsequent to being declared, custom operators are defined using standard function definition syntax:

```
infix operator <==> { precedence 130 associativity left }
func <==> (left: CGPoint, right: CGPoint) -> Bool {
  return left.x == right.x && left.y == right.y
}
let point1 = CGPoint(x: 1, y: 2)
let point2 = CGPoint(x: 1, y: 2)
println(point1 <==> point2) // Prints "true"
```

> **Tip** Overloading existing operators and creating new custom operators are powerful capabilities. It is generally advisable to carefully consider the obfuscation-to-benefit ratio before undertaking either action, especially for code that will be shared.

Blocks and Closure Expressions

Like Objective-C blocks, Swift closure expressions can be called inline, or stored and passed around to be executed at a later time. Both blocks and closure expressions can capture state, and they each deal similarly with avoiding strong reference cycles (a.k.a. retain cycles).

Table 6-6 compares the basic syntax of Objective-C blocks and Swift closure expressions.

***Table 6-6.** Basic syntax of Objective-C blocks and Swift closure expressions*

	Objective-C	Swift

Inline (anonymous)	`^(parameters) {`
	`  statements`
	`};`
		`{ (parameters) -> ReturnType in`
		`  statements`
		`}`

Stored	`ReturnType (^blockName)`
	`(ParameterTypes) =`
	`^(parameters) {`
	`  statements`
	`};`
		`let closureName = {`
		`(parameters) -> ReturnType in`
		`  statements`
		`}`

Objective-C blocks can use a `typedef` to help reduce the syntactic noise associated with declaring a block, whereas Swift closure expressions can adopt a variety of increasingly succinct syntax options that can result in incredibly concise yet expressive definitions. Table 6-7 demonstrates an Objective-C block compared to a series of Swift closure expressions ranging from explicit to terse, with setup code at the top and the output (common to all versions of the Swift examples) at the bottom. Notes on the Swift examples immediately follow the table.

Table 6-7. Comparing Objective-C blocks and Swift closure expressions

	Objective-C	Swift
	NSMutableArray *array = [@[@"Scott", @"Lori", @"Charlotte", @"Betty", @"Gracie", @"Sophie", @"Stella", @"Isabella", @"Lilith", @"Darby"] mutableCopy];	var array = ["Scott", "Lori", "Charlotte", "Betty", "Gracie", "Sophie", "Stella", "Isabella", "Lilith", "Darby"]

Explicit	[array sortUsingComparator:^
	NSComparisonResult(NSString
	*string1, NSString *string2) {
	  return [string1
	  compare:string2];
	}];
		sort(&array, { (s1:
		String, s2: String) ->
		Bool in
		  return s1 < s2
		})

Inferring parameter and return types		sort(&array, { s1, s2 in s1 < s2 })
Shorthand argument and trailing closure		sort(&array) { $0 < $1 }
Operator function		sort(&array, <)

	NSLog(@"%@", array); // Prints
	"(Betty, Charlotte, Darby,
	Gracie, Isabella, Lilith, Lori,
	Scott, Sophie, Stella)"
		println(array) // Prints
		"[Betty, Charlotte,
		Darby, Gracie, Isabella,
		Lilith, Lori, Scott,
		Sophie, Stella]"

Notes on the Swift examples in Table 6-6:

Explicit—The entire closure expression is enclosed in curly braces, and the start of the closure's body is signified by the in keyword.

Inferring parameter and return types—Because the closure is passed to the sort() function, the parameter and return types can be inferred from the sort() function's function type:

```
func sort<T>(inout array: [T], isOrderedBefore: (T, T) -> Bool)
```

This function type uses generic types, which will be covered in Chapter 11. Basically, this can be read as "The sort function of type T takes two parameters—a reference to an array variable (i.e., mutable) of type T, and a function that takes a tuple of two type T values and returns a Bool—and does not itself return a value." As demonstrated in this example, a single-expression closure can omit the `return` keyword.

Shorthand argument and trailing closure—Swift automatically creates incremental numbered argument names for incline closure expressions, that is, `$0`, `$1`, `$2`, and so on. Because these shorthand argument names can be used in lieu of declaring parameter names, the `in` keyword can also be omitted and the argument names used directly in the body of the expression. Notice also that when the last parameter of a function is a closure expression, that expression can be moved outside of the parentheses. Additionally, if the function does not take any other parameters, the parentheses can be omitted, too:

```
func someFunc(someOtherFunc: () -> NSTimeInterval) {
  println(someOtherFunc())
}
func getTimeInterval() -> NSTimeInterval {
  return NSDate.timeIntervalSinceReferenceDate()
}
someFunc(getTimeInterval) // Prints time interval, e.g., "431997792.008333"
```

Operator function—Swift defines several type-specific implementations of certain operators, such as the < and > operators that are implemented by an extension to `String` that conforms to the `Comparable` protocol (which, itself, conforms to the `_Comparable` protocol):

```
protocol _Comparable {
  func <(lhs: Self, rhs: Self) -> Bool
}
```

When these operator overloads are available, Swift can infer the parameters and return type from the function type of the operator function, and thus only the operator itself needs to be specified.

In Objective-C, the two most prominent scenarios in which a retain cycle can occur—wherein two objects hold a strong reference to each other and thus neither can ever be released and deallocated—are with storyboard outlet properties in the view controller, and when calling `self` within a block. Similarly, strong reference cycles can occur in Swift with outlet properties and between two reference types, such as two classes or a class and a closure expression. Working with storyboards and outlet properties is beyond the scope of this book. However, the latter situation will be addressed in the next chapter, alongside class reference types.

Declaration and Type Attributes

In a similar manner as stored values, function declarations can utilize declaration attributes to provide additional information about the function. See Chapter 2 for a list of available declaration attributes. Figure 6-2 demonstrates using the `@availability` declaration attribute with the `deprecated` and `message` attribute arguments to mark a function as deprecated and provide information about its replacement.

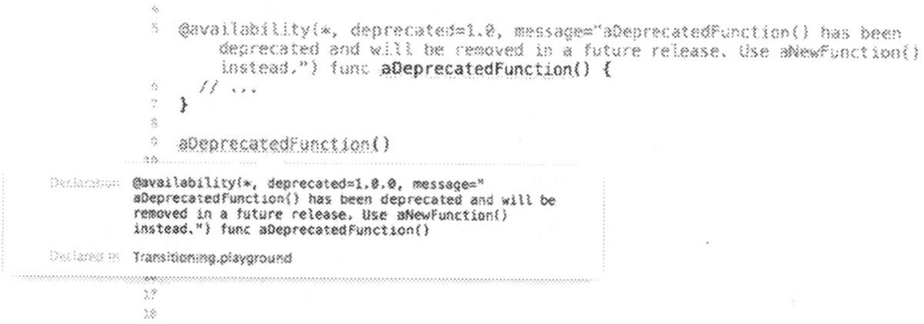

```
@availability(*, deprecated=1.0, message="aDeprecatedFunction() has been
    deprecated and will be removed in a future release. Use aNewFunction()
    instead.") func aDeprecatedFunction() {
    // ...
}

aDeprecatedFunction()
```

Declaration: @availability(*, deprecated=1.0.0, message="aDeprecatedFunction() has been deprecated and will be removed in a future release. Use aNewFunction() instead.") func aDeprecatedFunction()

Declared In: Transitioning.playground

***Figure 6-2.** Applying declaration attributes to a function in Swift*

Using the `obsoleted` attribute argument instead would generate a compiler error and prevent using the function, and also display a message if provided. Function types can apply type attributes including `@autoclosure` to implicitly enclose an expression in a closure, and `@noreturn` to specify that a function does not return to its caller:

```
func assertTruth(condition: @autoclosure () -> Bool) {
  if condition() {
  println("This is true")
} else {
  println("This is false")
  }
}
assertTruth(1 == 2) // Prints "This is false"
let swiftIsAwesome = true
assertTruth(swiftIsAwesome) // Prints "This is true"

@noreturn func fatalErrorHandler() {
  assert(false, "Oops!")
}
fatalErrorHandler() // assertion failed: Oops!
```

Summary

This chapter introduced you to one of Swift's most powerful features, closures, in the form of functions, nested functions, and closure expressions. Functions and closure expressions are most closely related to Objective-C methods and blocks, respectively, and thus comparative examples and approaches were provided throughout the chapter, along with tables summarizing syntax structures and mutability rules.

This chapter also kicks off the second half of this book, where we start to really dig into Swift's biggest game changers. As such, it represents a milestone turning point in your transition to programming in Swift, not just in syntax, but approach. Having followed along, typing in the sample code in a playground, REPL, or project, you may start to find yourself forgetting to type semicolons back in your Objective-C code, or inadvertently expecting Objective-C to infer your value types for you. And that's okay.

Chapter 7

Constructing Classes, Structures, and Enumerations

As alluded to in previous chapters, and revealed fully in this one, Swift breaks new ground with class types, and upgrades structures and enumerations to first-class status. In fact, there is less to say about the differences than similarities between classes and structures in Swift, and enumerations are not far off the mark, either. This chapter will introduce each of these constructs, first at a high level and then followed by deeper analysis of major considerations such as initialization, definition of properties and methods, and selection guidelines.

Naming Conventions

Swift follows the same naming conventions as Objective-C with regard to naming classes, structures, enumerations, properties, and methods. Classes, structures, and enumerations are all formal types, and thus their names should begin with a capital letter and use camel casing. Properties and methods are not types, so, in order to differentiate them from types, their names should begin with a lowercase letter and also use camel casing.

Classes and Structures

Objective-C classes are the workhorses of the language. From defining properties and methods to declaring protocols and calling on delegates, classes can satisfy a wide variety of needs. Objective-C is a superset of C and utilizes basic C structures as an alternative to classes. C structures are lighter-weight, although they are limited to storing scalar values (i.e., they cannot hold references to objects), and they cannot define methods.

Swift balances the workload between classes and structures, and as mentioned in Chapter 2, all of Swift's basic data types are implemented as structures (except Character, which is implemented as an enumeration). Table 7-1 compares classes and structures in Objective-C and Swift. Attributes are aligned horizontally to aid in cross-referencing.

Table 7-1. *Comparison of classes and structures in Objective-C and Swift*

	Objective-C	Swift
Class	Defines initializers Can define properties Can define instance variables Can define static variables Can implement custom deallocation logic	Defines initializers Can define stored instance properties Can define a deinitializer
	Can use lazy instantiation of properties Can define instance methods Can define class methods Almost always subclasses Can be subclassed Can have extensions and categories	Can define lazy stored properties Can define instance methods Can define type methods Can subclass Can be subclassed Can have extensions
	Can conform to protocols Can be type checked and casted Can define computed-property-like instance methods Can define computed-property-like class methods Can override property accessors	Can conform to protocols Can be type checked and casted Can define computed instance properties Can define computed type properties Can define property observers Can define subscripts
	Can have multiple references Passed by reference	Can have multiple references Passed by reference
Structure	Defines members	Defines stored instance properties

(continued)

Table 7-1. (*continued*)

Objective-C	Swift
Can define initializing functions Passed by copy	Has automatic memberwise initializers Passed by copy
	Can define stored type properties Can define computed instance properties Can define computed type properties Can define instance methods Can define type methods Can define subscripts Can have extensions Can conform to protocols

Although there seems to be general feature parity between Objective-C and Swift classes, it can be quickly deduced just by glancing over Table 7-1 that structures in Swift have many more capabilities. All of these similarities, differences, and new capabilities will be covered in the forthcoming sections.

Classes

There are three standout differences between classes in Objective-C and Swift:

1. Swift does not require creating separate interface and implementation files
2. Swift custom classes are not reliant on inheriting from a base class
3. Access control in Swift is entirely different

This chapter will cover the first two of these variances. Chapter 9 will deal with subclassing-specific topics, and Chapter 10 will analyze access control.

Objective-C's use of separate interface and implementation files has evolved over time, to the extent that many in the community have questioned the continued necessity of even having separate files. Swift answered that question: no, it's not necessary. Whereas class source files in Objective-C have a file extension of either `.h` or `.m`—for declaration and implementation code, respectively—all production source code files in Swift reside in a `.swift` file. In the case of Swift playgrounds, a `.playground` file is used.

Deferring the broader topic of access control for now, it is sufficient to understand here that the external interface for each Swift class (or structure) is made available to all other code within the module. Swift recognizes each build target in an Xcode project as a separate module, and modules can be imported. Table 7-2 compares the basic syntax of a class definition in Objective-C and Swift, absent of details for properties and methods, which will be covered later in this chapter. Optional components are italicized, and in order to keep these comparisons straightforward, accoutrements such as constants, macros, and extensions in Objective-C are omitted.

***Table 7-2.** Basic syntax of class definitions in Objective-C and Swift*

Objective-C	`// In .h interface file`
	`importStatements`
	`@interface ClassName : ParentClassName` *`<ProtocolName, ...>`*
	`publicPropertyDeclarations`
	`publicMethodDeclarations`
	`@end`
	`// In .m implementation file`
	`importStatements`
	`@implementation ClassName` *`<ProtocolName, ...>`*
	`{`
	   `instanceVariables`
	`}`
	`privatePropertyDeclarations`
	`methodImplementations`
	`@end`

Swift	`// In .swift file`
	`importStatements`
	`class ClassName:` *`ParentClassName, ProtocolName, ...`* `{`
	   `propertyDefinitions`
	   `methodDefinitions`
	`}`

Notice in the Swift example that defining a parent class is optional. Although it is technically also optional in Objective-C, most every class in Objective-C is a subclass of `NSObject`, for at least one reason: to inherit the `+[NSObject alloc]` method. Without that method, a class would have to implement its own memory allocation process and return an instance of the class to then be initialized. Classes in Swift are self-efficient with regard to the whole instantiation, initialization, and deinitialization process, inclusive of memory allocation. Also notice that a class in Swift may adopt one or more protocols, and protocols should be listed after the parent class (if there is one).

Structures

C structures in Objective-C facilitate storing scalar values, aggregates, or other structures as its members, and are passed by copy. Member values are normally retrieved and set using dot notation syntax, and although they can also be instantiated and referenced via structure pointers, this is less common in Objective-C programming where a class is typically used for anything but simple pass-by-copy data structures.

Table 7-3 compares the basic syntax of structure definitions in Objective-C and Swift; properties (and methods in Swift, which are optional) will be covered shortly.

***Table 7-3.** Basic syntax of structure definitions in Objective-C and Swift*

Objective-C	`typedef struct {`
	`   memberDeclarations`
	`} StructName;`

Swift	`struct StructName {`
	`   propertyDefinitions`
	`   methodDefinitions`
	`}`

Structures in Swift have been elevated to be nearly as capable as classes, with a few distinguishing differences that also help with determining whether to choose a class or structure for a particular need (selection guidelines are discussed later in this chapter in the section Selection Guidelines). The most notable differences between Swift structures and classes are:

- Classes can inherit from other classes. Structures cannot inherit from other structures (although they can conform to protocols)
- Structures have an automatically-generated *memberwise initializer* (covered later in this chapter); classes do not
- Structures can define both computed and stored type properties; classes can only define computed type properties
- Structures are value types, which are passed by copy; classes are reference types, which are passed by reference, and thus a single class instance can have multiple references

- Classes can be type checked and casted; because structures cannot inherit, they also cannot be type casted (and therefore, type checked)
- Classes can implement deinitializers to free up resources; structures cannot

Enumerations

Enumerations represent another chasm between Objective-C and Swift. Enumerations enable grouping related values together as a specific type of value. An enumeration can be iterated over (such as in a `switch` statement), and enumeration members can be passed as parameters to a function. Additionally, member names receive the benefit of code-completion, thus eliminating typo-related bugs that can be common when using raw strings. Enumerations are also commonly used with bitwise shift operators to combine multiple members into a single bitmask value, for example, for use in setting options in a method.

Objective-C utilizes straight C enumerations, adding helpful macros such as `NS_ENUM` and `NS_OPTIONS` that aid in defining new `typedef`'d enumerations. Members are named and represent differing, usually incremental, integer values (bitmasks in the case of `NS_OPTIONS`). Swift takes enumerations to a whole new level. One of the biggest differences is that Swift enumerations do not automatically assign a default integer value; member values are, by default, fully-fledged values of the enumeration type. Table 7-4 compares enumerations between Objective-C and Swift. Attributes are aligned horizontally to aid in cross-referencing.

Table 7-4. Comparison of enumerations in Objective-C and Swift

Objective-C	Swift
Defines members via comma-separated list	Defines members via case statements Can define multiple members in single case statement (comma-separated list)
Members defined with default integer value	Members are not automatically assigned a raw value Member default values are fully-fledged values of the enumeration type Member raw values can be a string, character, integer, or floating-point number

(continued)

Table 7-4. (*continued*)

Objective-C	Swift
Member values auto-increment if not explicitly assigned an integer value	If a raw integer value is assigned, subsequent member values auto-increment if not explicitly assigned an integer value Can define associated member values of any type and/or multiple types Can define initializers Can define computed instance properties Can define computed type properties Can define stored type properties Can define instance methods Can define type methods Can define subscripts Can have extensions Can conform to protocols Passed by copy

Table 7-5 compares the basic syntax of an enumeration definition in Objective-C and Swift; optional components are italicized.

***Table 7-5.** Basic syntax of enumeration definitions in Objective-C and Swift*

Objective-C	`typedef NS_ENUM(NSInteger, EnumName) {`
	   `value1 = `*`1`*`,`
	   `value2,`
	   `...`
	`};`

Swift	`enum Enum1Name {`
	   `case value1, `*`value2, ...`*
	   `init() { ... }`
	`}`
	`enum Enum2Name`*`: Int`*` {`
	   `case value1 = `*`1`*
	   `case value2`
	   `...`
	   `init() { ... }`
	`}`

Two versions of a Swift enumeration are included in Table 7-5, as individual enum members in Swift can be specified in individual case statements or in a single, comma-separated listed in one case statement.

Initialization

As already noted, Objective-C uses C-based structures and enumerations that do not have formal initializers (although initializer functions or factory methods could be created to vend initialized instances). Objective-C classes, along with Swift classes, structures, and enumerations, all define or inherit initializers that prepare an instance for use. The process of instantiation—which includes allocating the memory for an instance and then initializing it—is similar in outcome but significantly different in implementation between the two languages.

Class Initialization

Objective-C classes can define one or more initializers, typically with one designated initializer, that can optionally set default property values and perform other initialization tasks. Instantiating an Objective-C class instance involves first calling `+[<NSObject subclass> alloc]` to obtain an instance of the receiving class (memory allocated), and then passing that instance to an `-[<NSObject subclass> init]` method to complete initialization, or by calling a convenience class method such as `+[<NSObject subclass> new]` (which in turn simply calls `[[<NSObject subclass> alloc] init]`), or by calling any number of additional convenience constructors that may be available to receive a fully set up object back from a single method call that abstracts the `alloc`/`init` calls. This is an oversimplification of an elaborate process that has evolved over many years (Automatic Reference Counting, a.k.a. ARC, is one of the most profound improvements). Yet a comparison can now be made with how Swift handles class instantiation. Swift, also using ARC, handles all memory-management responsibilities associated with instantiating a class instance.

Swift classes must ensure that all nonoptional property values are set on initialization, and this is carried out by either setting default values in property declarations and/or in an initializer. Unlike Objective-C initializers, which return an initialized instance of the class, a Swift initializer's sole responsibility is to ensure that a new instance is properly set up before use.

> **Tip** A general best practice is to prefer setting a property's initial value in its declaration versus setting it in an initializer, whenever possible. This makes for more concise code, streamlines initializers, and benefits initializer inheritance (Chapter 9 will cover initializer inheritance in detail).

For base classes (i.e., that do not inherit from another class) wherein all nonoptional properties are assigned a default value during declaration, Swift automatically provides a *default initializer* that will set all the properties to their default values.

Initialization in Objective-C is typically carried out by assigning the response of a call to `-[super init]` (or a variation) to `self`, followed by (optionally) assigning initial values directly to the backing instance variables, and performing any other initialization tasks.

Swift defines two kinds of initializers: designated and convenience. *Designated initializers* are primarily responsible for ensuring that all of the class' properties are initialized. Every class must have at least one designated initializer, which can be inherited from a superclass (i.e., if the class has a superclass). Additionally, in the case in which there is a parent class, a designated initializer must also call a designated initializer in the immediate superclass; see Chapter 9 for details. *Convenience intitializers* are just that, initializers that conveniently abstract some of the work associated with initializing an instance of the class. They are optional, and marked with a `convenience` modifier before the `init` keyword in the function definition. A convenience initializer may call another convenience initializer or a designated initializer, for example, `self.init(parameterName: parameterValue)`. However, all convenience initializers must eventually point to a designated initializer. Apple's Swift language guide summarizes how designated and convenience initializers should be chained together, "Designated initializers must always delegate *up*. Convenience initializers must always delegate *across*."

Initialization in Swift is a two-phase process that is similar to initialization in Objective-C, except that Swift allows setting custom initial values in phase 1 versus in Objective-C, every property is initially assigned `0` or `nil`. In phase 1, memory is allocated, all nonoptional properties of the class are assigned an initial value, and the superclass (if one exists) is given the opportunity to assign values to all its nonoptional values (this repeats all the way up the inheritance chain). Essentially, phase 1 establishes `self`, which can then be accessed in phase 2 in order to further customize the instance. Table 7-6 provides examples of a basic class being defined and instantiated in Objective-C and Swift.

Table 7-6. Comparing definition and instantiation of a class in Objective-C and Swift

Objective-C

```
// In MyCustomClass.h
@import Foundation;
static NSString *defaultTitle = @"A Worthy Title";
@interface MyCustomClass : NSObject
@property (copy, nonatomic) NSString *title;
+ (instancetype)instanceWithDefaultTitle;
- (instancetype)initWithTitle:(NSString *)title;
@end
// In MyCustomClass.m
#import "MyCustomClass.h"
@implementation MyCustomClass
+ (instancetype)instanceWithDefaultTitle
{
   return [[MyCustomClass alloc] initWithTitle:nil];
}
- (instancetype)initWithTitle:(NSString *)title
{
   if (self = [super init]) {
      _title = title ?: defaultTitle;
   }
   return self;
}
@end
// In -[SomeOtherClass someMethod] in SomeOtherClass.m
MyCustomClass *myCustomClass1 = [MyCustomClass
instanceWithDefaultTitle]; // myCustomClass1.title =
"A Worthy Title"
MyCustomClass *myCustomClass2 = [[MyCustomClass alloc]
initWithTitle:@"A Great Title"]; // myCustomClass2.title =
"A Great Title"
```

(*continued*)

Table 7-6. (*continued*)

Swift	`// In .swift file`
	`class MyCustomClass {`
	`class var defaultTitle: String {`
	`   return "A Worthy Title"`
	`}`
	`var title: String!`
	`init(title: String) {`
	`   self.title = title`
	`}`
	`convenience init() {`
	`   self.init(title: MyCustomClass.defaultTitle)`
	` }`
	`}`
	`let myCustomClass1 = MyCustomClass() // myCustomClass1.title = "A Worthy Title"`
	`let myCustomClass2 = MyCustomClass(title: "A Great Title") // myCustomClass2.title = "A Great Title"`

Notice in the Swift example in Table 7-6 that the property `title` is of type `String!`. Remember from Chapter 2 that an ! can be used to implicitly unwrap an optional during declaration. In this example, the instances' `title` property is set during instantiation, however it can be subsequently set to `nil`, because it is an optional value. Observe also that the `init()` method automatically included the external `title` parameter name, even though it was not explicitly stated. As pointed out in the last chapter, Swift methods (functions defined within a type), automatically provide an external name for the second and subsequent parameters of a method. However, for `init()` methods, an external name is automatically provided for *all* parameters, including the first one.

> **Tip** To prevent an external name from automatically being created for an initializer parameter, write an underscore (_) before the parameter name, where an explicit external parameter name would normally be stated.

The use of `self` in the `init()` method was necessary to disambiguate the parameter from the property. Had the parameter been named `aTitle`, for example, the line setting the `title` property could have omitted using `self`, that is, `title = aTitle`. Also note that a computed type property was used, because, as of this writing, Swift does not support stored class properties; attempting to create one generates the compiler error: "class variables not yet supported."

Structure Initialization

As in Swift classes, Swift structure initializers must ensure that all nonoptional properties are set to an initial value, unless a property is set to a default value in its declaration.

When all nonoptional properties are assigned a default value in their declaration, a default initializer is automatically provided to set those initial values. Yet even when a structure does not set all of its nonoptional properties, if no custom initializer is defined, a *memberwise initializer* is automatically created, which essentially results in each property receiving an external name. That said, if a custom initializer is defined, neither a default initializer nor memberwise initializer will be available.

> **Tip** To regain access to the default initializer for a structure that declares one or more custom initializers but also sets default values for all nonoptional properties, simply define an empty initializer:
>
> ```
> init() {}
> ```

Table 7-7 demonstrates the definition, instantiation, and usage of a structure in Objective-C and Swift.

***Table 7-7.** Comparing definition, instantiation, and usage of a structure in Objective-C and Swift*

Objective-C	`typedef struct {`
	`char *date;`
	`char *message;`
	`NSInteger value;`
	`} MyStruct;`
	`MyStruct myStruct1 = { "9/9/14", "Hello iPhone", 6 };`
	`MyStruct myStruct2 = { .message = "goodbye iPhone",`
	`.value = 5 };`
	`NSLog(@"%s: %s %li, %s %li", myStruct1.date,`
	`myStruct1.message, (long)myStruct1.value, myStruct2.message,`
	`(long)myStruct2.value); // Prints "9/9/14: Hello iPhone 6,`
	`goodbye iPhone 5"`

(continued)

Table 7-7. (*continued*)

Swift	`struct MyStruct {`
	`  static let date = "9/9/14"`
	`  var message = "Hello iPhone"`
	`  var value = 6`
	`  init() {}`
	`  init(message: String, value: Int) {`
	`    self.message = message`
	`    self.value = value`
	`  }`
	`}`
	`let myStruct1 = MyStruct()`
	`var myStruct2 = MyStruct(message: "goodbye iPhone", value: 5)`
	`println("\(MyStruct.date): \(myStruct1.message) \(myStruct1.value), \(myStruct2.message) \(myStruct2.value)") // Prints "9/9/14: Hello iPhone 6, goodbye iPhone 5"`

Enumeration Initilialization

Enumerations are comparatively simple to define and instantiate in both Objective-C and Swift, as Table 7-8 demonstrates.

Table 7-8. Comparing definition and instantiation of an enumeration in Objective-C and Swift

Objective-C	`typedef NS_ENUM(NSInteger, MyEnum) {`
	`  value1, value2, value3`
	`};`
	`MyEnum myEnum = value1;`
	`NSLog(@"%i", myEnum); // Prints 0`
	`typedef NS_OPTIONS(NSInteger, MyOptionsEnum) {`
	`  v1 = 1 << 0,`
	`  v2 = 1 << 1,`
	`  v3 = 1 << 2`
	`};`
	`MyOptionsEnum myOptionsEnum = v3;`
	`NSLog(@"%i", myOptionsEnum); // Prints 4`

(*continued*)

Table 7-8. (*continued*)

Swift	<pre>enum MyEnum1 {
	  case value1, value2, value3
	}
	var myEnum1 = MyEnum1.value1
	println(_stdlib_getDemangledTypeName(myEnum1)) // Prints
	"...MyEnum1"
	myEnum1 = .value2
	println(_stdlib_getDemangledTypeName(myEnum1)) // Prints
	"...MyEnum1"
	enum MyEnum2: Int {
	  case value1 = 1, value2, value3
	  init() {
	    self = value3
	  }
	}
	var myEnum2 = MyEnum2()
	println(myEnum2.rawValue) // Prints "3"
	myEnum2 = .value1
	println(myEnum2.rawValue) // Prints "1"</pre>

In the Swift examples, notice that MyEnum1 does not define a type, referred to as the *raw value* type for enumerations, whereas MyEnum2 defines that it has a raw value of type Int. As pointed out in Table 7-4, MyEnum1 values are of type MyEnum1. Swift enumeration member raw values must be literal, which means it is not possible to use bitwise shifting to assign values (as in the NS_OPTIONS example). The raw value of a Swift enumeration that defines a raw value can be accessed via the read-only rawValue property. Also notice that enumeration values can be assigned using short dot syntax (instead of explicitly stating the type, e.g., MyEnum.value1), because the type can already be inferred.

Failable Initializers

Under certain circumstances, such as when a required external resource is not available during initialization or an invalid parameter value is passed to an initializer, initialization may fail. One or more *failable initializers* can be defined for a class, structure, or enumeration, in order to handle the possibility that initialization may not succeed. As previously mentioned, a Swift initializer does not return an instance of the type but, rather, it ensures that all nonoptional property values are set. A failable initializer, however, will either succeed and result in the creation of a fully-initialized *optional* value of the type, or it will fail and must *explicitly* return nil.

To define an initializer as failable, write a ? immediately after the `init` keyword. As with other uses of optional values, an instance initialized with a failable initializer must be unwrapped before using. That said, a failable initializer may also be defined such that it will result in the creation of an implicitly unwrapped optional instance. To define an implicitly unwrapped failable initializer, write an ! immediately after the method name.

> **Note** Failable or not, an initializer cannot be defined with the same parameter names and types as another existing initializer for the same type.

The Swift standard library automatically defines the failable initializer `init?(rawValue:)` for enumerations defined as having a raw value. Table 7-9 provides examples of failable initializers for classes, structures, and enumerations.

Table 7-9. Examples of class, structure, and enumeration failable initializers in Swift

<table>
<tr><td>Class</td><td><pre>
class Person {
  let firstName: String!
  let lastName: String!
init?(firstName: String, lastName: String) {
  if firstName.isEmpty || lastName.isEmpty {
    return nil
  }
  self.firstName = firstName
  self.lastName = lastName
  }
}
let noOne = Person(firstName: "", lastName: "")
println(noOne) // Prints "nil"
let vivian = Person(firstName: "Vivian", lastName:
"Gardner")
println("\(vivian!.firstName) \(vivian!.lastName)")
// Prints "Vivian Gardner"
</pre></td></tr>
</table>

(*continued*)

Table 7-9. (*continued*)

Structure	`struct Polygon {`
	`let sides: Int!`
	`init!() {`
	`    sides = 5`
	`}`
	`init?(sides: Int) {`
	`    if sides < 3 { return nil }`
	`    self.sides = sides`
	`  }`
	`}`
	`let pentagon = Polygon()`
	`println(pentagon.sides) // Prints "5"`
	`let hectogon = Polygon(sides: 100)`
	`if let sides = hectogon?.sides {`
	`  println(sides)`
	`}`
	`// Prints "100"`

Enumeration	`import Foundation`
	`enum AirPressure: String {`
	`    case Hectopascals = "inHg"`
	`    case Millibars = "mb"`
	`    var value: Double! {`
	`    // API call that gets current air pressure in`
	`    hectopascals, e.g., 30 inHg`
	`    let currentAirPressure = 30.0`
	`    switch self {`
	`    case .Hectopascals:`
	`    return currentAirPressure`
	`case .Millibars:`
	`    return currentAirPressure * 33.8637526`
	`  }`
	`}`

(*continued*)

Table 7-9. (*continued*)

```
var reading: String {
   let roundedValue = String(format: "%.1f", value)
   return "\(roundedValue) \(self.rawValue)"
  }
init?(_ unit: String) {
   if unit.isEmpty { return nil }
   if let airPressure = AirPressure(rawValue: unit) {
   self = airPressure
} else {
   return nil
  }
 }
}
var airPressure = AirPressure("mb")
println(airPressure!.reading) // Prints "1015.9 mb"
airPressure = .Hectopascals
println(airPressure!.reading) // Prints "30.0 inHg"
```

Properties

Both Objective-C and Swift classes can store values as properties, yet Swift structures and enumerations can also have properties. Table 7-10 itemizes the kinds of properties each Swift construct can define.

Table 7-10. Itemizing available property types for classes, structures, and enumerations in Swift

	Stored Instance	Computed Instance	Stored Type	Computed Type
Class	✓	✓		✓
Structure	✓	✓	✓	✓
Enumeration		✓	✓	✓

Stored type properties are marked with the `static` keyword in the definition. Computed type properties are marked with the `class` keyword for classes, and `static` keyword for structures and enumerations.

Properties in Objective-C are typically defined with explicit memory retention and atomicity rules, whereas in Swift, all value types (i.e., structures and enumerations) are copy, and all reference types (e.g., classes) are strong. There is one exception to this rule, which will be covered in the section Declaration and Type Attributes. Of atomicity, Apple states to use, "...`dispatch_once` to make sure that the initialization is atomic.," (`https://developer.apple.com/swift/blog/?id=7`). An example of when this exception would be necessary will be demonstrated in the section Singletons.

Swift properties are regular stored or computed values of a class, structure, or enumeration, declared as variables or constants within the class, structure, or enumeration. Although Objective-C properties are automatically synthesized with backing instance variables, no such construct exists in Swift. The backing store of a Swift property is not directly accessible, and access to a property's value is facilitated via the getter and setter of that property. A Swift property with only a getter is read-only, just like an Objective-C property with the `readonly` property attribute.

Stored type properties in Swift can be set (if declared as a variable) and retrieved on a structure or enumeration type itself, just like instance properties. This is similar to static variables (mutable) and constants (immutable) in Objective-C, except that static variables and constants are accessed directly instead of as properties of the class using dot notation, as they are in Swift.

> **Note** Stored type properties must always be given an initial value, since there is no initializer to set them.

A property can be lazily instantiated in Objective-C by overriding the getter and working directly with the backing instance variable for the property. Swift has *lazy stored properties* (variable stored properties marked with the `lazy` modifier) that achieve the same goal of delaying calculation of a property's initial value until the first time it is retrieved.

> **Note** Constant properties in Swift must be set during declaration or in an initializer and cannot be marked as `lazy`.

Swift computed properties can be retrieved and set (if variable) like a regular stored property, but return a computed value or process a set value (such as to indirectly set other properties), respectively. A computed property can optionally have only a getter and setter, and when it has only a getter, the `get` keyword can be omitted. A computed setter can specify a parameter name for the new value, enclosed in parentheses after the `set` keyword. If no parameter name is specified *and the parentheses* are omitted, a default `newValue` parameter name is automatically created and made available for use.

A Swift property can be initialized using a closure, which is similar to using a block within a custom getter in Objective-C. Keep in mind that, during initialization, the instance has not yet been fully initialized, so other properties should not be accessed in the closure, nor should `self` be accessed or any other methods called. In order to execute the closure immediately, write `()` immediately following the closing curly brace of the closure.

Changes to a Swift property can also be observed via a property observer. Property observers respond to changes in a property's value by calling the `willSet` and `didSet` and passing along the new or old value, accordingly. Similar to computed properties, if a parameter name is not specified in parentheses following the implementation of a `willSet` or `didSet` method, a parameter name of `newValue` or `oldValue`, respectively, is automatically created.

> **Note** `willSet` and `didSet` are not called during initialization, nor are they called if the property is changed within either method. However, they are called even if the property is set to a new value that is equal to the current value.

In Objective-C, public methods can be used to achieve an effect similar to Swift computed properties, and public property accessors can be overridden to provide Swift's property-observer-like handling of changes to a property's value.

Table 7-11 provides examples of each of the aforementioned property types in Objective-C and Swift. To keep the comparison clear-cut, the Objective-C computed instance example does not include type checking, which would be necessary for production code. An example of using a block or closure to initialize a property will be included in Chapter 9.

Table 7-11. Examples of property definitions in Objective-C and Swift

	Objective-C	Swift
Stored instance	@property (copy, nonatomic) NSString *title;	var title: String!

Computed instance	// In HttpStatusChecker.h
	@import Foundation;
	@interface HttpStatusChecker : NSObject
	+ (instancetype)checkerWithHttpStatus:(NSArray *)
	httpStatus;
	- (NSArray *)status;
	- (void)setStatus:(NSArray *)httpStatus;
	@end
	// In HttpStatusChecker.m
	#import "HttpStatusChecker.h"
	@interface HttpStatusChecker ()
	@property (assign, nonatomic) NSInteger code;
	@property (copy, nonatomic) NSString *message;
	@end
	@implementation HttpStatusChecker
	+ (instancetype)checkerWithHttpStatus:(NSArray
	*)httpStatus
	{
	HttpStatusChecker *status = [HttpStatusChecker new];
	[status setStatus:httpStatus];
	return status;
	}
		struct HttpStatusChecker {
		var code: Int!
		var message: String!
		var status: (Int, String) {
		get {
		return (code, message)
		}
		set {
		code = newValue.0
		message = newValue.1
		}
		}
		init(status: (Int, String)) {
		code = status.0
		message = status.1
		}
		}
		var httpStatusChecker =
		HttpStatusChecker(status: (200, "OK"))
		println("code: \(httpStatusChecker.
		status.0), status: \(httpStatusChecker.
		status.1)") // Prints "code: 200, status:
		OK"

```
- (instancetype)init
{
  if (self = [super init]) {
    _code = 200;
    _message = @"OK";
  }
  return self;
}
- (NSArray *)status
{
  return @[@(self.code), self.message];
}
- (void)setStatus:(NSArray *)httpStatus
{
  self.code = [(NSNumber *)httpStatus[0] integerValue];
  self.message = httpStatus[1];
}
@end
// In -[SomeOtherClass someMethod] in SomeOtherClass.m
HttpStatusChecker *httpStatusChecker = [HttpStatusChecker
checkerWithHttpStatus:@[@200, @"OK"]];
NSLog(@"code: %@, status: %@", httpStatusChecker.
status[0], httpStatusChecker.status[1]); // Prints "code:
200, status: OK"
```

(continued)

Table 7-11. (continued)

	Objective-C	Swift
Stored class/type	`static NSString *defaultTitle = @"A Worthy Title";`	`// In structure or enumeration` `static var defaultTitle = @"A Worthy Title"`

Computed class/type	`// In DateChecker.h`
	`@import Foundation;`
	`@interface DateChecker : NSObject`
	`+ (NSString *)dateString;`
	`@end`
	`// In DateChecker.m`
	`#import "DateChecker.h"`
	`@implementation DateChecker`
	`+ (NSString *)dateString`
	`{`
	`    return [NSDateFormatter localizedStringFromDate:[NSDate date] dateStyle:NSDateFormatterShortStyle timeStyle:NSDateFormatterNoStyle];`
	`}`
	`@end`
	`// In -[SomeOtherClass someMethod] in SomeOtherClass.m`
	`NSLog(@"%@", [DateChecker dateString]); // Prints current date, e.g., "9/14/14"`
		`class DateChecker {`
		`  class var dateString: String {`
		` return NSDateFormatter.localizedStringFromDate(NSDate(), dateStyle: .ShortStyle, timeStyle: .NoStyle)`
		`  }`
		`}`
		`println(DateChecker.dateString) // Prints current date, e.g., "9/14/14"`

Observer

```
// In TitleTracker.h
@import Foundation;
@interface TitleTracker : NSObject
@property (copy, nonatomic) NSString *title;
@property (assign, nonatomic) BOOL isBeingInstantiated;
+ (instancetype)trackerWithTitle:(NSString *)title;
@end
// In TitleTracker.m
#import "TitleTracker.h"
@interface TitleTracker ()
@property (copy, nonatomic) NSString *oldTitle;
@end
@implementation TitleTracker
+ (instancetype)trackerWithTitle:(NSString *)title
{
    TitleTracker *tracker = [TitleTracker new];
    tracker.isBeingInstantiated = YES;
    tracker.title = title;
    tracker.isBeingInstantiated = NO;
    return tracker;
}
```

```
class TitleTracker {
  var title: String! {
    willSet {
      print("'\(newValue)'
      (fka '\(title)'). ")
    }
    didSet {
      println("Farewell to
      '\(oldValue).'")
    }
  }
  init(title: String) {
    self.title = title
  }
}
let myTitleTracker = TitleTracker(title:
"A Worthy Title")
myTitleTracker.title = "A Better Title" //
Prints "'A Better Title' (fka 'A Worthy
Title'). Farewell to 'A Worthy Title.'"
```

(continued)

Table 7-11. (continued)

Objective-C	Swift

```
- (void)setTitle:(NSString *)title
{
    if (!self.isBeingInstantiated) {
        const char* oldTitle = [self.oldTitle UTF8String];
        printf("'%s' (fka '%s'). Farewell to '%s.'\n",
        [title UTF8String], oldTitle, oldTitle);
        title = title;
    }
    self.oldTitle = title;
}
@end
// In -[SomeOtherClass someMethod] in SomeOtherClass.m
TitleTracker *myTitleTracker = [TitleTracker
trackerWithTitle:@"A Worthy Title"];
myTitleTracker.title = @"A Better Title"; // Prints "'A
Better Title' (fka 'A Worthy Title'). Farewell to 'A
Worthy Title.'"
```

Enumeration Associated Values

Swift enumerations can also associate passed-in values to its members. Each enumeration `case` can be assigned the passed in value, and value types can be of any type and even different between `case`s. Associated values can also be extracted in a `switch` statement using value binding:

```
enum BookID {
  case isbn10(Int)
  case isbn13(String)
  case oclc(String)
  case lccn(String)
  case olid(String)
  var title: String! {
    var t: String!
    switch self {
      // Simulating setting t via API call or query
    case let .isbn10(id):
      t = "Transitioning to Swift"
    case let .isbn13(id):
      t = "Transitioning to Swift"
    case let .oclc(id):
      t = "Transitioning to Swift"
    case let .lccn(id):
      t = "Transitioning to Swift"
    case let .olid(id):
      t = "Transitioning to Swift"
    }
    return t
  }
}
let bookId = BookID.isbn10(1484204077)
println(bookId.title) // Prints "Transitioning to Swift"
```

Subscripts

Objective-C classes can add array- or dictionary-like subscripting by overriding `-objectAtIndexedSubscript:` and/or `-setObject:forKeyedSubscript:`, taking a key (and object) to get (or set) an object, respectively. In Swift, classes, structures, and enumerations can all define subscripts that can take multiple input parameters and/or a variadic parameter, be multidimensional (same as collection types), be read-write or read-only (using getters and setters, just like computed properties), return any value type (including multiple values in a tuple), and can even be overloaded. They cannot, however, use inout parameters to modify pass-by-reference parameters, nor can they define default parameter values:

```
class Introspector {
  var values: Any!
  subscript(theValues: Int...) -> (sum: Int, average: Double) {
    values = theValues
      var sum = 0
      for integer in theValues {
        sum += integer
      }
      let average = Double(sum) / Double(theValues.count)
      return (sum: sum, average: average)
  }
  subscript(theValues: Double...) -> (sum: Double, average: Double) {
    values = theValues
      var sum = 0.0
      for value in theValues {
        sum += Double(value)
      }
      let average = sum / Double(theValues.count)
      return (sum: sum, average: average)
  }
}
let myIntrospector = Introspector()
let result1 = myIntrospector[1, 2, 3, 4, 5]
println("For \(myIntrospector.values), sum is \(result1.sum) and average is
\(result1.average).") // Prints "For [1, 2, 3, 4, 5], sum is 15 and average
is 3.0."
let result2 = myIntrospector[1.1, 2.2, 3.3, 4.4, 5.5]
println("For \(myIntrospector.values), sum is \(result2.sum) and average is
\(result2.average).") // Prints "For [1.1, 2.2, 3.3, 4.4, 5.5], sum is 16.5
and average is 3.3."
```

Methods

In Objective-C, only classes can define methods, which can either be instance or class methods. In Swift, classes, structures, and enumeration can all define methods, including both instance and type methods. Swift methods are simply functions that are associated to a specific type.
For example, initializers are instance methods (in both Objective-C and Swift). Remember from the last chapter that parameters of functions (and thus methods) are constants by default; explicitly declare a parameter as a variable by using the var prefix. Objective-C methods are called on instances and classes using bracket notation. Swift methods use the same dot syntax to call methods as to access properties.

Write the keyword `static` before the method name for structure and enumeration type methods, and write the `class` keyword for class type methods. As mentioned previously, Swift methods automatically provide an external name for the second and subsequent parameters when calling the method. Figure 7-1 compares the same function as a global function and as a method within a class.

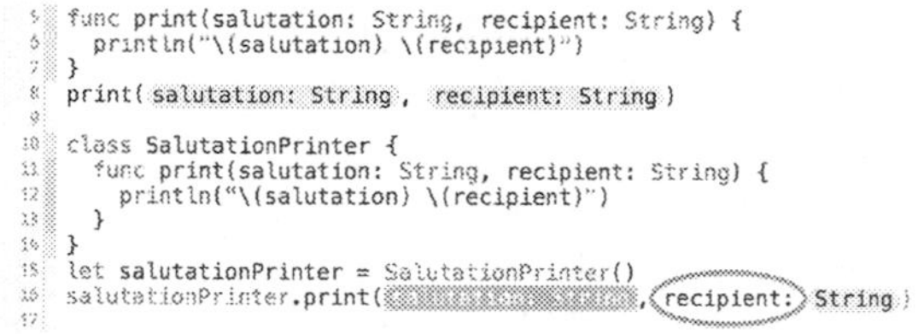

```
func print(salutation: String, recipient: String) {
  println("\(salutation) \(recipient)")
}
print( salutation: String , recipient: String )

class SalutationPrinter {
  func print(salutation: String, recipient: String) {
    println("\(salutation) \(recipient)")
  }
}
let salutationPrinter = SalutationPrinter()
salutationPrinter.print( salutation: String , recipient: String )
```

***Figure 7-1.** Comparing a global function to method in Swift*

Presumably, the intention of this additional feature of methods over regular functions is to maintain the style of Objective-C method inline parameter names and general self-documenting readability. Although the examples in Figure 7-1 demonstrate this difference, good form would actually be to provide an explicit external name for the second parameter, as demonstrated in Table 7-13.

When calling an instance method within another instance method within that same type, it is not necessary to explicitly state `self`. The same goes for calling a type method within another type method of the same type:

```
struct Incrementor {
  static var value = 0
  static func increment(_ increment: Int = 1) {
    value++
    println(value)
  }
  init() {
    printCurrentValue()
  }
  func printCurrentValue() {
    println("Current value: \(Incrementor.value)")
  }
```

```
  func topLevelFunc() {
    func nestedFunc() {
      printCurrentValue()
    }
    nestedFunc()
  }
}
Incrementor.increment()   // Prints "1"
Incrementor.increment()   // Prints "2"
var typer = Incrementor() // Prints "Current value: 2"
typer.topLevelFunc()      // Prints "Current value: 2"
```

Notice in this example that it is not necessary to specify `Incrementor` for `value` in `increment()`, nor is it necessary to specify `self` for `printCurrentValue()` in `init()`, or in the nested function `nestedFunction()`, yet it is necessary to specify `Incrementor.value` in `printCurrentValue()`, because that is an instance function accessing a type property.

By default, instance properties of value types cannot be changed from within their own instance methods. Because enumerations cannot have instance properties, this rule applies only to structures. To opt in to the *mutating behavior* of an instance method, such that it can change instance property values and write back those changes when the method ends, write the `mutating` keyword before the `func` keyword in the definition. A mutating method in Swift can even instantiate a completely new instance of that type and assign it to `self`, which is not possible in Objective-C. Class instance properties, as well as type properties of value types (i.e., structures and enumerations) can be mutated within the type's instance methods.

Table 7-12 provides examples of Objective-C methods and Swift functions, specific to the unique features of methods over functions as described in this section; the Objective-C method calls are being made within `-[SomeOtherClass someMethod]` in `SomeOtherClass.m`. Refer to the last chapter for more detailed coverage of Swift functions in general.

Table 7-12. Comparing unique features of Swift methods over functions to Objective-C methods

	Objective-C	Swift

	// In SalutationPrinter.h
	@import Foundation;
	@interface SalutationPrinter :
	NSObject
	+ (void)print:(NSString *)
	salutation toRecipient:(NSString
	*)recipient;
	- (void)print:(NSString *)
	salutation toRecipient:(NSString
	*)recipient;
	@end
	// In SalutationPrinter.m
	#import "SalutationPrinter.h"
	@implementation SalutationPrinter
	+ (void)print:(NSString *)
	salutation toRecipient:(NSString
	*)recipient
	{
	NSLog(@"%@ %@", salutation,
	recipient);
	}
	- (void)print:(NSString *)
	salutation toRecipient:(NSString
	*)recipient
	{
	NSLog(@"%@ %@", salutation,
	recipient);
	}
	@end
		class SalutationPrinter {
		class func
		print(salutation: String,
		toRecipient recipient:
		String) {
		println("\(salutation)
		\(recipient)")
		}
		func print(salutation:
		String, toRecipient
		recipient: String) {
		println("\(salutation)
		\(recipient)")
		}
		}
		struct Counter {
		var total = 0
		var reset: Bool = false
		mutating func increment()
		{
		if reset {
		self = Counter()
		}
		total++
		println(total)
		}
		}

Instance method	SalutationPrinter
	*salutationPrinter =
	[SalutationPrinter new];
	[salutationPrinter print:@"Hello"
	toRecipient:@"Henry"]; // Prints
	"Hello Henry"
		let salutationPrinter =
		SalutationPrinter()
		salutationPrinter.
		print("Hello", toRecipient:
		"Henry") // Prints "Hello
		Henry"

(continued)

Table 7-12. (*continued*)

	Objective-C	Swift
Class/type method	`[SalutationPrinter print:@"Hello" toRecipient:@"Henry"]; // Prints "Hello Henry"`	`SalutationPrinter.print("Hello", toRecipient: "Henry") // Prints "Hello Henry"`

Mutating instance method	N/A	`var counter = Counter()`
		`counter.increment()`
		`// Prints "1"`
		`counter.increment()`
		`// Prints "2"`
		`counter.reset = true`
		`counter.increment()`
		`// Prints "1"`

Declaration and Type Attributes

Swift classes can utilize declaration attributes just like stored values and functions to provide additional information:

```
@availability(iOS, obsoleted=1.0, message="Use NewIOSClass instead")
class OldIOSClass { /* ... */ }
@availability(iOS, introduced=0.8)
class NewIOSClass { /* ... */ }
// Originally implemented in release 0.1
@availability(*, introduced=0.1)enum MyStruct { /* ... */ }
// Renamed in release 1.0
@availability(*, introduced=1.0, renamed="MyRenamedStruct") enum
MyRenamedStruct { /* ... */ }
typealias MyStruct = MyRenamedStruct
```

In these examples, `OldIOSClass` is an iOS-only class that was obsoleted in 1.0, and its usage will be prevented by a compiler error; it was replaced by `NewIOSClass` in 0.8 (and, presumably, from 0.8 to 1.0, `OldIOSClass` was marked `deprecated`). `MyStruct` was renamed in 1.0 to `MyRenamedStruct`, and a `typealias` is used to ensure existing code will still work with the old name.

As previously stated, reference types properties in Swift have strong memory retention by default. However, reference type properties marked with the declaration attribute `@NSCopying` will have their setter synthesized with a copy of the passed in value, similar to how the copy property attribute works in Objective-C. That property's type must also conform to the `NSCopying` protocol; protocols are covered in the next chapter.

Although the topic of mixing Objective-C and Swift source files in the same project is beyond the scope of this book, there is one declaration attribute use case specific to classes that should be mentioned here. The `@objc` attribute can be used to mark a class as available to Objective-C source code within the same module. An *Xcode-generated header* must also be imported within an Objective-C source code file in order to expose the Swift source code files to it. The generated header file has the name *`ProductModuleName`*`-Swift.h`, where *`ProductModuleName`* is the name of the target. When exposing a Swift class to Objective-C code, a different name can be provided for use by the Objective-C code by placing that name in parentheses immediately after the @objc attribute. And for classes marked with the @objc attribute, individual entities within that class can have different names exposed to Objective-C by marking those entities with the @objc attribute.

> **Note** Swift classes that are intended to be made available to Objective-C code should subclass `NSObject` in order to inherit `+[NSObject alloc]`.

```
// In SwiftClass.swift
import Foundation
@objc class MySwiftCustomClass: NSObject {
  var enabled: Bool
  init(enabled: Bool) {
    self.enabled = enabled
    super.init()
  }
}

// In SomeOtherClass.m
#import "Transitioning-Swift.h"
@implementation SomeOtherClass
- (void)someMethod
{
  MySwiftCustomClass *swiftClassInstance = [[MySwiftCustomClass alloc]
initWithEnabled:NO];
}
```

> **Note** Apple provides a useful guide for mixing Swift and Objective-C code in the same project, which includes listing Swift-only features that are not accessible within a class or protocol marked with the @objc attribute: *Using Swift with Cocoa and Objective-C* (`http://bit.ly/mixswiftandobjc`).

See Chapter 2 and the last chapter for a list of additional declaration attributes and examples. Swift classes, structures, and enumerations can use `autoclosure` and `noreturn` type attributes in their method declarations in the same manner as described in the last chapter for using type declarations with functions.

Class Deinitialization

Deinitialization in Swift applies only to class types, and is similar to deallocation in Objective-C, except that deinitialization is what happens right *before* a Swift class get deallocated. Because of this, a *deinitializer* in Swift has full access to its instance, including all its properties. A class can have at most only a single deinitializer, which is defined as a `deinit` method that takes no parameters and, uniquely, is written without parentheses. `deinit` is automatically called right before deallocation and should not be called directly. Although the topic of subclasses is deferred until Chapter 9, it should be mentioned here that a subclass inherits its superclass' deinitializer, and the superclass' deinitializer is automatically called at the end of the subclass' deinitialization, even if an explicit `deinit` method was not defined for the class. Swift automatically deallocates an instance when it is no longer referenced (via ARC), so explicitly defining `deinit` is not generally necessary unless some manual process or cleanup must be performed right before deallocation. Table 7-13 compares a common use case for `-[NSObject dealloc]` in Objective-C and `deinit` in Swift.

Table 7-13. Comparing use of `-[NSObject dealloc]` *in Objective-C and* `deinit` *Swift*

Objective-C	<pre>// In KeyboardDisplayHandler.h
	@import UIKit;
	@interface KeyboardDisplayHandler : NSObject
	@end
	// In KeyboardDisplayHandler.m
	#import "KeyboardDisplayHandler.h"
	@implementation KeyboardDisplayHandler
	- (instancetype)init
	{
	  if (self = [super init]) {
	    NSNotificationCenter *notificationCenter =
	    [NSNotificationCenter defaultCenter];
	    [notificationCenter addObserver:self selector:
	    @selector(keyboardWillShow) name:UIKeyboardWillShow
	    Notification object:nil];
	    [notificationCenter addObserver:self selector:
	    @selector(keyboardWillHide) name:UIKeyboardWillHide
	    Notification object:nil];
	    }
	  return self;
	}
	- (void)keyboardWillShow
	{
	  // ...
	}
	- (void)keyboardWillHide
	{
	  // ...
	}
	@end</pre>

(*continued*)

Table 7-13. (*continued*)

Swift	`class KeyboardDisplayHandler {`
	`  init() {`
	`    NSNotificationCenter.defaultCenter().addObserver(self,`
	`    selector: "keyboardWillShow",`
	`    name: UIKeyboardWillShowNotification, object: nil)`
	`    NSNotificationCenter.defaultCenter().addObserver(self,`
	`    selector: "keyboardWillHide",`
	`    name: UIKeyboardWillHideNotification, object: nil)`
	`  }`
	`  func keyboardWillShow() {`
	`    // ...`
	`  }`
	`  func keyboardWillHide() {`
	`    // ...`
	`  }`
	`  deinit {`
	`    NSNotificationCenter.defaultCenter().removeObserver(self)`
	`  }`
	`}`

Avoiding Strong Reference Cycles

Because Swift classes are reference types, and thus a single class instance can have multiple (default strong) references to it, a situation can occur where two class instances can hold a strong reference to each other, such that neither will ever be deallocated. This is a strong reference cycle, a familiar situation to Objective-C developers. And the approach to avoid a strong reference cycle between classes in Swift is similar to the approach taken in Objective-C.

In Swift, a *weak reference* must be declared as optional variables, as their value must be able to be set to `nil` during runtime. By contrast, an *unowned reference* in Swift always will have a value and cannot be set to `nil`.

> **Tip** If a class will *always* have a reference to another class, mark the property that points to an instance of that other class as `unowned`. Otherwise, if the class may not always have a reference to another class, mark the property as `weak`.

Table 7-14 provides comparative examples of avoiding strong reference cycles in Objective-C and Swift.

> **Tip** Swift playgrounds do not consistently call `deinit`. As such, while the `println()` statements in the example code in Tables 7-14 and 7-15 would print out if run in an Xcode project, they may not print out when run in a playground.

***Table 7-14.** Avoiding strong reference cycles in Objective-C and Swift*

Objective-C

```
// In MyCustomClass.h
@import Foundation;
@class ParkingSpaceAssignment;
@interface Employee : NSObject
@property (strong, nonatomic) ParkingSpaceAssignment
*parkingSpaceAssignment;
@end
@interface ParkingSpace : NSObject
@property (assign, nonatomic) NSUInteger number;
@property (weak, nonatomic) ParkingSpaceAssignment *assignment;
- (instancetype)initWithNumber:(NSUInteger)number;
@end
@interface ParkingSpaceAssignment : NSObject
@property (weak, nonatomic) ParkingSpace *parkingSpace;
@property (weak, nonatomic) Employee *employee;
- (instancetype)initWithParkingSpace:(ParkingSpace *)
parkingSpace employee:(Employee *)employee;
@end
// In MyCustomClass.m
#import "MyCustomClass.h"
@implementation Employee
- (void)dealloc
{
  NSLog(@"Fired!");
}
@end
@implementation ParkingSpace
- (instancetype)initWithNumber:(NSUInteger)number
{
  if (self = [super init]) {
    _number = number;
  }
  return self;
}
- (void)dealloc
{
  NSLog(@"Parking space deleted");
}
@end
```

(continued)

Table 7-14. (*continued*)

	`@implementation ParkingSpaceAssignment`
	`- (instancetype)initWithParkingSpace:(ParkingSpace *)`
	`parkingSpace employee:(Employee *)employee`
	`{`
	`  if (self = [super init]) {`
	`    _parkingSpace = parkingSpace;`
	`    _employee = employee;`
	`  }`
	`  return self;`
	`}`
	`- (void)dealloc`
	`{`
	`  NSLog(@"Assignment deleted");`
	`}`
	`@end`
	`// In -[SomeOtherClass someMethod] in SomeOtherClass.m`
	`Employee *chris = [Employee new];`
	`ParkingSpace *parkingSpace = [[ParkingSpace alloc]`
	`initWithNumber:8];`
	`chris.parkingSpaceAssignment = [[ParkingSpaceAssignment`
	`alloc] initWithParkingSpace:parkingSpace employee:chris];`
	`chris = nil;`
	`/* Prints:`
	`Fired!`
	`Assignment deleted`
	`*/`

Swift	`class Employee {`
	`  weak var parkingSpaceAssignment: ParkingSpaceAssignment?`
	`  init() { }`
	`  deinit {`
	`    parkingSpaceAssignment = nil`
	`    println("Fired!")`
	`  }`
	`}`
	`class ParkingSpace {`
	`  let number: Int`
	`  weak var assignment: ParkingSpaceAssignment?`
	`  init(number: Int) {`
	`    self.number = number`
	`  }`
	`}`

(*continued*)

Table 7-14. (*continued*)

```
class ParkingSpaceAssignment {
  unowned var parkingSpace: ParkingSpace
  unowned var employee: Employee
  init(parkingSpace: ParkingSpace, employee: Employee) {
    self.parkingSpace = parkingSpace
    self.employee = employee
  }
  deinit {
    println("Assignment deleted")
  }
}
var chris: Employee? = Employee()
var parkingSpace = ParkingSpace(number: 8)
chris!.parkingSpaceAssignment = ParkingSpaceAssignment
(parkingSpace: parkingSpace, employee: chris!)
chris = nil
/* Prints:
Assignment deleted
Fired!
*/
```

In Objective-C, capturing `self` in a block will also result in a strong reference cycle, because blocks maintain a strong reference to any captured objects, including `self`. A similar situation can also occur in Swift that results in a strong reference cycle. Closures are reference types, just like classes. So, if a closure that is assigned to a property in a class instance calls `self` in any way, such as to access another property or call a method, a strong reference cycle will occur.

> **Note** To help avoid creating a strong refence cycle, Swift requires explicitly stating `self` within a closure, such as `self.someProperty` or `self.someMethod()`.

The solution in Objective-C is to create a weak reference to self ahead of and for use in the block.

Swift, by contrast, employs *closure capture lists*. A closure can define a capture list as part of its overall definition, to specify if one or more captures should be handled as weak or unowned references. As with nonclosure properties, a weak reference must always be declared as an optional variable.

> **Tip** If the capture can be set to nil, such as if the instance it references gets deallocated, define the capture as weak. Otherwise, if a closure and a capture within that closure will *always* refer to each other and be deallocated at the same time, define the capture as unowned.

The syntax to define a capture list is to enclose a rule (or multiple rules in a comma-separated list) inside square brackets, within the closure body, after the opening curly brace and typically on the next line, before the closure's parameter list and return value (if provided and cannot be inferred), followed by the in keyword. A rule consists of the weak or unowned keyword followed by a *single* capture. The basic syntax is as follows:

```
lazy var someClosure: (ParamType, ...) -> ReturnType = {
  [weak self] (paramOneName: ParamType, ...) -> ReturnType in
  statements
}
```

An arbitrary expression can also be bound to a named value in a capture list, as demonatrated in Table 7-15, which compares how to avoid strong reference cycles in Objective-C blocks and Swift closure properties of a class instance.

Table 7-15. Avoiding strong reference cycles in Objective-C blocks and Swift closure properties of a class instance

Objective-C

```
// In MyCustomClass.h
@import Foundation;
@interface Bravo : NSObject
@property (copy, nonatomic) NSString *value;
- (instancetype)initWithValue:(NSString *)value;
@end
@interface Charlie : NSObject
@property (copy, nonatomic) NSString *value;
- (instancetype)initWithValue:(NSString *)value;
@end
typedef void (^Printer)();
@interface Alpha : NSObject
@property (copy, nonatomic) NSString *value;
@property (strong, nonatomic) Bravo *bravo;
@property (strong, nonatomic) Charlie *charlie;
@property (copy, nonatomic) Printer printOutValues;
- (instancetype)initWithValue:(NSString *)value
bravoValue:(NSString *)bravoValue charlieValue:(NSString *)
charlieValue;
@end
// In MyCustomClass.m
#import "MyCustomClass.h"
@implementation Bravo
- (instancetype)initWithValue:(NSString *)value
{
  if (self = [super init]) {
    _value = value;
  }
  return self;
}
- (void)dealloc
{
  NSLog(@"Bravo deallocated");
}
@end
```

(continued)

Table 7-15. (*continued*)

```
@implementation Charlie
- (instancetype)initWithValue:(NSString *)value
{
  if (self = [super init]) {
    _value = value;
  }
  return self;
}
- (void)dealloc
{
  NSLog(@"Charlie deallocated");
}
@end
@implementation Alpha
- (instancetype)initWithValue:(NSString *)value
bravoValue:(NSString *)bravoValue charlieValue:(NSString *)
charlieValue
{
  if (self = [super init]) {
    _value = value;
    _bravo = [[Bravo alloc] initWithValue:bravoValue];
    _charlie = [[Charlie alloc] initWithValue:charlieValue];
    __weak typeof(self)weakSelf = self;
      _printOutValues = ^{
        if (weakSelf.value.length && weakSelf.bravo.value.
        length && weakSelf.charlie.value.length) {
           NSLog(@"%@ %@ %@", weakSelf.value, weakSelf.bravo.
           value, weakSelf.charlie.value);
        }
      };
  }
  return self;
}
- (void)dealloc
{
    NSLog(@"Alpha deallocated");
}
@end
```

(*continued*)

Table 7-15. (*continued*)

	`// In -[SomeOtherClass someMethod] in SomeOtherClass.m`
	`Alpha *alpha = [[Alpha alloc] initWithValue:@"Alpha"`
	`bravoValue:@"Bravo" charlieValue:@"Charlie"];`
	`alpha.printOutValues(); // Prints "Alpha Bravo Charlie"`
	`alpha.bravo = nil;      // Prints "Bravo deallocated"`
	`alpha.charlie = nil;    // Prints "Charlie deallocated"`
	`alpha = nil;            // Prints "Alpha deallocated"`

Swift	`class Bravo {`
	`  var value: String`
	`  init(_ value: String) {`
	`    self.value = value`
	`  }`
	`  deinit {`
	`    println("Bravo deallocated")`
	`  }`
	`}`
	`class Charlie {`
	`  var value: String`
	`  init(_ value: String) {`
	`    self.value = value`
	`  }`
	`  deinit {`
	`    println("Charlie deallocated")`
	`  }`
	`}`
	`class Alpha {`
	`  var value: String`
	`  var bravo: Bravo?`
	`  var charlie: Charlie?`
	`  lazy var printOutValues: () -> () = {`
	`    [unowned self, weak bravo = self.bravo, weak charlie =`
	`    self.charlie] in`
	`    if bravo != nil && charlie != nil {`
	`      println("\(self.value) \(bravo!.value)`
	`      \(charlie!.value)")`
	`    }`
	`  }`

(*continued*)

Table 7-15. (*continued*)

```
  init(value: String, bravoValue: String, charlieValue: String) {
    self.value = value
    bravo = Bravo(bravoValue)
    charlie = Charlie(charlieValue)
  }
  deinit {
  println("Alpha deallocated")
  }
}
var alpha: Alpha? = Alpha(value: "Alpha", bravoValue:
"Bravo", charlieValue: "Charlie")
alpha?.printOutValues() // Prints "Alpha Bravo Charlie"
alpha!.bravo = nil      // Prints "Bravo deallocated"
alpha!.charlie = nil    // Prints "Charlie deallocated"
alpha = nil             // Prints "Alpha deallocated"
```

Singletons

In the same blog post cited earlier referencing atomicity in Swift, Apple further states that the initializer for global variables and for static members of structures and enumerations is run on first access, using `dispatch_once` from GCD (Grand Central Dispatch being right up there with ARC as a major milestone addition to the platform) to ensure the initialization is atomic. With that said, Table 7-16 compares creating singletons in Objective-C and Swift (credit goes to Stack Overflow user "David" for the elegant Swift example he provided: `http://stackoverflow.com/a/24073016/616764`).

Table 7-16. Comparing creation of singletons in Objective-C and Swift

<table>
<tr><td>Objective-C</td><td><pre>// In StoreManager.h
@import Foundation;
@interface StoreManager : NSObject
+ (instancetype)sharedManager;
@end
// In StoreManager.m
#import "StoreManager.h"
@implementation StoreManager
+ (instancetype)sharedManager
{
  static StoreManager *sharedManager = nil;
  static dispatch_once_t onceToken;
  dispatch_once(&onceToken, ^{
    sharedManager = [StoreManager new];
  });
  return sharedManager;
}
@end
// In -[SomeOtherClass someMethod] in SomeOtherClass.m
StoreManager *sharedStoreManager1 = [StoreManager
sharedManager];
StoreManager *sharedStoreManager2 = [StoreManager
sharedManager];
NSLog(@"%@", sharedStoreManager1 == sharedStoreManager2 ?
@"YES" : @"NO"); // Prints "YES"</pre></td></tr>
<tr><td>Swift</td><td><pre>class StoreManager {
  class var sharedManager: StoreManager {
    struct Manager {
      static let instance = StoreManager()
    }
    return Manager.instance
  }
}
let sharedStoreManager1 = StoreManager.sharedManager
let sharedStoreManager2 = StoreManager.sharedManager
println(sharedStoreManager1 === sharedStoreManager2)
// Prints "true"</pre></td></tr>
</table>

Selection Guidelines

Eumerations offer many new capabilities in Swift, such that an enumeration could actually handle a need that would normally be served by a class or structure. For example, an enumeration could be used to capture state that has nothing to do with an actual sequence of related values. In the spirit of the old adage, “Just because you can does not necessarily mean you should,” an enumeration should really only be chosen when an enumeration is needed. The new capabilities afforded enumerations in Swift should be taken advantage of in conjunction with satisifying an enumerative need, not in lieu of choosing a more appropriate type when there is no such need.

The near-feature parity nature of classes and structures in Swift can make choosing one over the other more of a challenge. While there are certainly going to be use cases where it won’t really matter which type is used, Table 7-17 offers some basic guidelines to help discern when one really is a better choice over the other for a particular need.

Table 7-17. *Guidelines for selecting a class or structure in Swift*

	Class	Structure
Needs to inherit certain capabilities, initially or perceivably later	✓	
Needs to be able to be inherited from	✓	
May need to be type casted	✓	
Needs to store type properties to be shared with all instances		✓
Needs broadest range of storage options (i.e., stored and computed instance and type properties)		✓
Needs to store simple values		✓
Needs to store large values	✓	
May need to perform some final process or do manual cleanup before being deallocated	✓	
Will only ever need to be copied when passed around in code (e.g., to a function)		✓
Should be referenced when passed (e.g., to a function)	✓	
Needs to be a singleton instance	✓	
Needs to (optionally) conform to optional protocols	✓	

All of these guidelines are based on topics covered thus far, except optional protocols, which will be introduced in Chapter 8.

Summary

In this chapter, the differences between Objective-C and Swift classes, structures, and enumerations—of which there are many—and the similarities between Swift classes, structures, and enumerations—of which there are also many—were examined. Copious examples and tables summarizing rules and features were provided to accompany narrative explanations in an effort to expose sometimes subtle distinctions. Additionally, selection guidelines were introduced to help choose the best tool for the task at hand.

Chapter 8

Defining and Adopting Protocols

Swift is predominantly a protocol-based language. Protocols are also prevalent in Objective-C, frequently used with the delegation design pattern—although there has been a gradual shift from protocol/delegate to block-based usage in recent years. A protocol is simply a contract that defines requirements that the adopting type agrees to implement. This chapter will compare how Objective-C and Swift similarly utilize protocols, pointing out the differences in syntax and examining the broadened usage, new capabilities, and specific caveats of using protocols in Swift.

Use Cases

Protocols are used similarly in Objective-C and Swift to set the expected behavior of a class or type. A protocol accomplishes this by declaring property and/or method requirements that a class or type adopting the protocol must conform to, unless the requirement is optional. Only classes can adopt protocols in Objective-C, whereas in Swift, classes, structures, and enumerations can all adopt protocols. Objective-C protocols can have one or more sections marked as optional, and any requirements declared in an optional section are in fact not required but can optionally be implemented by the adopting class if need be. Swift protocol requirements can also be made optional; however, conformance to a protocol with one or more optional requirements is limited to classes in Swift. For Swift structures and enumerations, protocols can mutate the underlying instance of a type that conforms to the protocol.

In both Objective-C and Swift, protocols can be used with the delegation pattern to allow a class or structure to assign the responsibility of conforming to a protocol to an instance of another type, without needing to know anything more about that instance or its type. In Swift, protocols themselves can also be used as abstract types in most places where a type would typically be used, to state that the type of the instance conforms to the protocol. Examples include declaring the type of a stored value or collection of stored values, or a parameter or return value type of a function.

Protocols in both Objective-C and Swift can adopt other protocols. However, unlike in Objective-C, where a protocol can adopt a protocol and redeclare a method to make it optional, Swift protocols cannot change the optionality of an inherited requirement.

In Swift, types can be type checked for conformance to a protocol, and a type that conforms to a protocol can be type casted as that protocol, which has the effect of limiting its capabilities to that which are defined in the protocol for the scope of that cast (but the type is not actually changed in any way).

Naming

As with all types, protocol names should be camel cased, beginning with a capital letter. Although there are no hard and fast rules for how to name protocols, protocol names should generally be descriptive of their requirements. Examples include `HasName` or `Named` for a `name` property requirement, `Tappable` for a requirement to handle taps, `SomeTypeDelegate` when the responsibility of conforming to the requirements will be handed off to a conforming delegate instance, and `SomeTypeDataSource` when the requirement is to provide a source of data. And like all types, protocols can be `typealias`'d:

```
typealias ThatLongProtocol = SomeReallyLongProtocolNameThatIHaveToUseALot
```

Defining

Table 8-1 compares the basic layout of a protocol declaration in Objective-C and Swift.

Table 8-1. Basic layout of protocol declarations in Objective-C and Swift

Objective-C	`// In .h interface file`
	`@protocol ProtocolName <NSObject, AdditionalProtocolName, ...>`
	`propertyDefinitions`
	`methodDefinitions`
	`@end`

Swift	`protocol ProtocolName: AdditionalProtocolName, ... {`
	`  propertyDefinitions`
	`  methodDefinitions`
	`}`

Objective-C protocols declare adoption of additional protocols within angle brackets, whereas Swift uses the same colon syntax as with explicitly declaring stored value types or parent types.

The syntax of property and method declarations in an Objective-C protocol is exactly the same as property and method declaration syntax, such as in an interface file or an extension—although it hasn't been necessary to declare private methods in an extension since the introduction of the two-pass LLVM compiler in Xcode 3.1. Coincidentally, the author of the LLVM project, Chris Lattner, is also the original developer of Swift (`http://nondot.org/sabre/`).

Just as Objective-C protocols can declare both class and instances methods, Swift protocols can declare both type and instance methods. The syntax for declaring a method in a Swift protocol looks like a regular function definition, but without the curly braces and method body. Swift protocol methods cannot declare default values; however, they can declare a variadic parameter (see Chapter 6 for details). Type methods are prefixed with the `class` keyword, and classes implementing a protocol type method also use the `class` keyword prefix. However, structures and enumerations that implement a protocol type method continue to use the `static` keyword prefix.

A Swift protocol can require a property and specify whether the property should provide a getter, or a getter and a setter; that is, it must always provide a getter. It cannot specify whether the property should be stored or computed, and because this cannot be determined by the declaration alone, protocol properties must be declared as variables in order to (potentially) be able to satisfy the requirement that a computed property cannot be a constant. The syntax to declare a protocol property is the same as declaring a regular property with an explicit type, followed by `{ get }` or `{ get set }` to indicate the getter or getter and setter requirements, respectively.

Objective-C protocol methods are required by default, although any methods declared after an `@optional` directive are, in fact, optional (the `@required` directive can be used to explicitly state the required nature of methods can are declared after it, or to switch back to required method declarations after an optional section, although it is considered good form to list all the required methods first, followed by an `@optional` directive and then optional methods). Within Swift protocols, optional requirements are marked with an `optional` modifier prefix, and whenever one or more of its requirements are marked optional, the entire protocol must be initially prefixed with the `@objc` attribute. Only classes in Swift can adopt a protocol containing optional requirements, that is, structures and enumerations cannot adopt `@objc` protocols.

Table 8-2 provides examples of protocol declarations in Objective-C and Swift.

***Table 8-2.** Example protocol declarations in Objective-C and Swift*

Objective-C

```
// In .h interface file
@import Foundation;
@protocol Protocol <NSObject>
@property (copy, nonatomic) NSString *requiredProperty;
- (void)requiredMethod;
@optional
@property (assign, nonatomic) NSInteger optionalProperty;
- (void)optionalMethod;
@end
```

Swift

```
protocol RequiredProtocol: AnotherProtocol {
  var requiredProperty: String { get set }
  func requiredMethod()
}
@objc protocol PartiallyOptionalProtocol {
  var requiredProperty: String { get set }
  func requiredMethod()
  optional var optionalProperty: Int { get set }
  optional func optionalMethod()
}
```

Although it is a best practice in Objective-C for a protocol to minimally declare that it inherits from the base `NSObject` protocol (which `NSObject`, the class, also conforms to), Swift protocols are free to inherit from one or more protocols, or not. Two examples of Swift protocols were provided to be able to separately demonstrate the required use of the `@objc` attribute for a protocol that contains optional requirements. Only a class could adopt `PartiallyOptionalProtocol`, whereas a class, structure, or enumeration could adopt `RequiredProtocol`, as long as it also conforms to the `AnotherProtocol` that `RequiredProtocol` inherits from.

Just as an Objective-C protocol can declare adopting one or more additional protocols, Swift protocols can inherit from one or more protocols. One stipulation is that, although `@objc` protocols cannot inherit from non-`@objc` protocols, non-`@objc` protocols *can* inherit from `@objc` protocols. However, the same rule applies that structures and enumerations cannot adopt `@objc` protocols, nor can they adopt a non-`@objc` protocol that inherits from an `@objc` protocol:

```
@objc protocol Protocol1 {
  // ...
}
protocol Protocol2: Protocol1 {
  // ...
}
```

Protocols can also apply declaration and type attributes. The following examples also include adoption of the protocols, which is covered in the next section:

```
protocol CanHandleFatalError {
  @noreturn func fatalErrorHandler()
}
struct ErrorHandler: CanHandleFatalError {
  @noreturn func fatalErrorHandler() {
    assert(false, "Oops!")
  }
}
let errorHandler = ErrorHandler()
errorHandler.fatalErrorHandler() // assertion failed: Oops!

protocol CanTellTheTruth {
  func assertTruth(condition: @autoclosure () -> Bool)
}
class TruthTeller: CanTellTheTruth {
  func assertTruth(condition: @autoclosure () -> Bool) {
    if condition() {
      println("This is true")
    } else {
      println("This is false")
    }
  }
}
let truthTeller = TruthTeller()
truthTeller.assertTruth(1 == 2) // Prints "This is false"
let swiftIsAwesome = true
truthTeller.assertTruth(swiftIsAwesome) // Prints "This is true"
```

Adopting

Objective-C classes and Swift types declare adoption of protocols the same way protocols declare adoption of other protocols, that is, via a single protocol or comma-separated list of protocols, enclosed in angle brackets in Objective-C, or after the type name and a colon in Swift.

> **Note** Swift classes that inherit from a parent class and adopt one or more protocols should list the parent class first, and then the protocol(s), in a comma-separated list.

Objective-C classes can declare protocol adoption in either the interface (`.h`) or an extension within the implementation (`.m`) files. Protocol adoption in Swift is declared in the type definition itself.

A Swift type can also declare adoption of multiple protocols using a *protocol composition*, which is a temporary local protocol that has the combined requirements of all the protocols in the composition. The syntax of a protocol composition is `protocol<Protocol1, Protocol2, ...>`.

In Objective-C, properties and variables of type `id` can declare conformance to one or more protocols, using the syntax `id<Protocol1, Protocol2, ...>`. Swift stored values can also be declared as of one or more protocol types, in which case, the type of the stored value must conform to the protocol(s). Arrays, dictionaries, and tuples can also declare that they are of one or more protocol types.

> **Note** A Swift dictionary requires its key to conform to the `Hashable` protocol, which inherits from `Equatable`. Conforming to `Equatable` requires implementing the equality operator (==), which requires two concrete values, which is not possible to do in a protocol declaration. The solution is to create a structure of type `Hashable` that acts as a wrapper around a value of any type that conforms to `Hashable`, that is passed in to be used as a key when creating a new instance of the structure. The structure's type can then be used as the key type when explicitly declaring the key and value types for a dictionary variable or constant. A more detailed explanation and the actual code are available in a blog post by a member of the Swift compiler team at `https://devforums.apple.com/message/1045616`.

The syntax for a stored value declaring adoption of a single protocol is the same as when explicitly declaring a type. A protocol composition must be used for a stored value to declare adoption of two or more protocols.

Table 8-3 provides example snippets to demonstrate and compare the syntax for declaring protocol adoption by classes, types, and instances. Note that AnyKey in the Swift dictionary example is the type of a structure that conforms to Hashable, as described in the aforementioned Note.

Table 8-3. *Examples of classes, types, and instances declaring protocol adoption in Objective-C and Swift*

	Objective-C	Swift
Class	`@interface CustomClass : NSObject <Protocol1, Protocol2>`	`class CustomClass: ParentClass, Protocol1, Protocol2 { // ... }`
Structure	`N/A`	`struct CustomStruct: Protocol1, Protocol2 { // ... }`
Enumeration	`N/A`	`enum CustomEnum: Int, Protocol1, Protocol2 { // ... }`
Single stored value	`id<Protocol1, Protocol2> delegate;`	`var storedValue1: Protocol1` `var storedValue2: protocol<Protocol1, Protocol2>`

Collection	`N/A`	`var array1: [Protocol1]`
		`var array2: [protocol<Protocol1, Protocol2>]`
		`var dictionary1: [AnyKey: Protocol1]`
		`var dictionary2: [AnyKey: protocol<Protocol1, Protocol2>]`

Tuple	`N/A`	`var tuple1: (Protocol1, Protocol2)` `var tupel2: (Protocol1, protocol<Protocol2, Protocol3>)`
Property	`@property (strong, nonatomic) id<Protocol1, Protocol2> delegate;`	`Same syntax as for a single stored value, collection, or tuple`

Table 8-4 compares protocol adoption and conformace by classes in Objective-C and Swift.

> **Note** The `Printable` protocol used in Tables 8-4 and 8-5 is meant for demonstrative purposes only, as the Swift standard library already includes a `Printable` protocol:
>
> ```
> protocol Printable {
>     var description: String { get }
> }
> ```

Table 8-4. Comparing class protocol adoption in Objective-C and Swift

Objective-C	Swift
`// In CustomClass.h`	`protocol HasString {`
`@import Foundation;`	`  var string: String { get set }`
`@protocol HasString <NSObject>`	`}`
`@property (copy, nonatomic) NSString`	`protocol Printable: HasString {`
`*string;`	`  func printString()`
`@end`	`}`
`@protocol Printable <NSObject,`	`@objc protocol HasReversedString {`
`HasString>`	`  var reversedString: String { get }`
`- (void)printString;`	`  optional func`
`@end`	`  printReversedString()`
`@protocol HasReversedString <NSObject>`	`}`
`@property (copy, nonatomic) NSString`	`protocol IsPalindromic {`
`*reversedString;`	`  var isPalindromic: Bool { get }`
`@end`	`}`
`@protocol IsPalindromic <NSObject>`	`protocol MakePalindromic {`
`@property (assign, nonatomic) BOOL`	`  mutating func`
`isPalindromic;`	`  convertToPalindrome()`
`@end`	`}`

(*continued*)

Table 8-4. (*continued*)

Objective-C	Swift

`@interface CustomClass : NSObject`
`<Printable, HasReversedString,`
`IsPalindromic>`
`@property (copy, nonatomic) NSString`
`*string;`
`@property (copy, nonatomic) NSString`
`*reversedString;`
`@property (assign, nonatomic) BOOL`
`isPalindromic;`
`- (void)printString;`
`- (void)printReversedString;`
`@end`
`// In CustomClass.m`
`#import "CustomClass.h"`
`@implementation CustomClass`
`- (instancetype)init`
`{`
`  if (self = [super init]) {`
`    _string = @"AManAPlanACanalPanama";`
`  }`
`  return self;`
`}`
`- (NSString *)reversedString`
`{`
`  NSMutableString *reversedString =`
`  [@"" mutableCopy];`
`  [self.string enumerateSubstrings`
`  InRange:NSMakeRange(0, self.string.`
`  length) options:(NSStringEnumeration`
`  Reverse|NSStringEnumerationBy`
`  ComposedCharacterSequences)`
`  usingBlock:^(NSString *substring,`
`  NSRange substringRange, NSRange`
`  enclosingRange, BOOL *stop) {`
`    [reversedString`
`    appendString:substring];`
`  }];`
`  _reversedString = reversedString;`
`  return _reversedString;`
`}`
	`class CustomClass: Printable,`
	`HasReversedString, IsPalindromic {`
	`  var string: String =`
	`  "AManAPlanACanalPanama"`
	`  var reversedString: String {`
	`    let reversedValueArray =`
	`    reverse(string)`
	`    return`
	`    "".join(reversedValueArray.map`
	`    { String($0) })`
	`  }`
	`  var isPalindromic: Bool {`
	`    return string.lowercaseString`
	`    == reversedString.`
	`    lowercaseString`
	`  }`
	`  init () { }`
	`  init(string: String) {`
	`    self.string = string`
	`  }`
	`  func printString() {`
	`    println(string)`
	`  }`
	`  func printReversedString(){`
	`    println(reversedString)`
	`  }`
	`}`
	`var printableValue: CustomClass =`
	`CustomClass()`
	`printableValue.printReversedString()`
	`// Prints "amanaPlanaCAnalPAnaMA"`
	`println(printableValue.isPalindromic)`
	`// Prints "true"`

(*continued*)

Table 8-4. (*continued*)

Objective-C	Swift

`- (BOOL)isPalindromic`
`{`
`  return [self.string.lowercaseString`
`  isEqualToString:self.`
`  reversedString.lowercaseString];`
`}`
`- (void)printString`
`{`
`  NSLog(@"%@", self.string);`
`}`
`- (void)printReversedString`
`{`
`  NSLog(@"%@", self.reversedString);`
`}`
`@end`
`// In -[SomeOtherClass someMethod] in`
`SomeOtherClass.m`
`CustomClass *printableValue =`
`[CustomClass new];`
`[printableValue printReversedString];`
`// Prints "amanaPlanaCAnalPAnaMA"`
`NSLog(@"%@", printableValue.`
`isPalindromic ? @"YES" : @"NO");`
`// Prints "YES"`	

As mentioned in the last chapter, reference type properties marked with the declaration attribute @NSCopying will have their setter synthesized with a copy of the passed in value, similar to the way in which the copy property attribute works in Objective-C. That property's type must also conform to the NSCopying protocol:

```
import Foundation
class CopyingClass: NSCopying {
  func copyWithZone(zone: NSZone) -> AnyObject {
    return CopyingClass()
  }
}
```

```
class ClassWithProperties {
  var nonCopyingProperty: CopyingClass {
    didSet {
      println("self.nonCopyingProperty === oldValue: \(self.
nonCopyingProperty === oldValue)")
    }
  }
  @NSCopying var copyingProperty: CopyingClass {
    didSet {
      println("self.copyingProperty === oldValue: \(self.copyingProperty ===
oldValue)")
    }
  }
  init(nonCopyingProperty: CopyingClass, copyingProperty: CopyingClass) {
    self.nonCopyingProperty = nonCopyingProperty
    self.copyingProperty = copyingProperty
  }
}
let copyingClass = CopyingClass()
let classWithProperties = ClassWithProperties(nonCopyingProperty:
copyingClass, copyingProperty: copyingClass)
classWithProperties.nonCopyingProperty = copyingClass // Prints "self.
nonCopyingProperty === oldValue: true"
classWithProperties.copyingProperty = copyingClass // Prints "self.
copyingProperty === oldValue: false"
```

Table 8-5 provides examples of structure and enumeration protocol adoption and conformance in Swift (using the protocol declarations from Table 8-4).

Table 8-5. Examples of structure and enumeration protocol adoption in Swift

Structure	`struct CustomStruct: IsPalindromic, MakePalindromic {`
	`  var valuesArray: [CustomClass]`
	`  var isPalindromic: Bool {`
	`    var isPalindromic = true`
	`    let lastIndex = valuesArray.endIndex - 1`
	`    let halfCount = Int(valuesArray.count / 2)`
	`    for i in 0..<halfCount {`
	`      let x = valuesArray[i].string`
	`      let y = valuesArray[lastIndex - i].string`
	`      if x != y {`
	`        isPalindromic = false`
	`        break`
	`      }`
	`    }`
	`    return isPalindromic`
	`  }`
	`  mutating func convertToPalindrome() {`
	`    if !isPalindromic {`
	`      var reversedArray = reverse(valuesArray)`
	`      valuesArray = valuesArray + reversedArray`
	`    }`
	`    let valuesString = " ".join(valuesArray.map {`
	`    "[\($0.string)]" })`
	`      println(valuesString)`
	`  }`
	`}`
	`let alpha = CustomClass(string: "Alpha")`
	`let bravo = CustomClass(string: "Bravo")`
	`let charlie = CustomClass(string: "Charlie")`
	`let delta = CustomClass(string: "Delta")`
	`let foxtrot = CustomClass(string: "Foxtrot")`
	`var customStruct: protocol<IsPalindromic,`
	`MakePalindromic> = CustomStruct`
	`(valuesArray: [alpha, bravo, charlie,`
	`delta, foxtrot])`
	`println(customStruct.isPalindromic)`
	`// Prints "false"`
	`customStruct.convertToPalindrome()`
	`// Prints "[Alpha] [Bravo] [Charlie]`
	`[Delta] [Foxtrot] [Foxtrot] [Delta]`
	`[Charlie] [Bravo] [Alpha]"`
	`println(customStruct.isPalindromic) // Prints "true"`

(continued)

Table 8-5. (*continued*)

Enumeration	<pre>enum CustomEnum: Int, Printable {
	  case One = 1, Two, Three
	  var string: String {
	    get {
	      var value: String
	      switch self {
	        case .One:
	          value = "One"
	        case .Two:
	          value = "Two"
	        case .Three:
	          value = "Three"
	      }
	      return value
	    }
	    set {
	      let value = newValue.toInt() ?? 1
	      self = CustomEnum(rawValue: value)!
	    }
	  }
	  func printString() {
	    println(string)
	  }
	}
	var customEnum = CustomEnum.One
	customEnum.string = "a"
	customEnum.printString() // Prints "One"</pre>

Objective-C categories and extensions can be used to declare adoption of one or more protocols by an existing class—and provide the conforming implementation in the case of categories. Swift extensions can be used similarly for these purposes, which will be covered in the next chapter.

Type Checking and Casting

The `is`, `as`, and `as?` operators (covered in Chapter 4) can be used to check for conformance to, or cast as, a protocol, respectively. Usage is exactly the same as when type checking or casting to a nonprotocol type. However, only protocols marked with the `@objc` attribute can be type checked, and thus, only classes in Swift can be type checked or casted to. When casting to a protocol type, the underlying value is not actually changed in any way, but is simply treated as a type having the properties and methods defined by the protocol for the scope of that cast. This is the same behavior as when casting nonprotocol types (covered in Chapter 4):

```
@objc protocol HasTitle {
  var title: String { get set }
}
@objc protocol HasPageCount {
  var pageCount: Int { get set }
  optional var title: String { get set }
}
class Book: HasTitle, HasPageCount {
  var title: String
  var pageCount: Int
  var tableOfContents: String!
  init(title: String, pageCount: Int) {
    self.title = title
    self.pageCount = pageCount
    tableOfContents = "\tTable Of Contents\n\t..."
  }
  func goToChapter(chapter: Int) {
    // ...
    println("Going to chapter \(chapter)")
  }
}
class Article: HasTitle, HasPageCount {
  var title: String
  var pageCount: Int
  init(title: String, pageCount: Int) {
    self.title = title
    self.pageCount = pageCount
  }
}
class Video: HasTitle {
  var title: String
  init(title: String) {
    self.title = title
  }
}
let book = Book(title: "Transitioning to Swift", pageCount: 200)
let article = Article(title: "How to Perform a Lightweight Core Data
Migration", pageCount: 25)
let video = Video(title: "How To Use Xcode Behaviors")
let publishedWorks: [HasTitle] = [book, article, video]
for item in publishedWorks {
  if let printItem = item as? HasPageCount {
    let pageString = printItem.pageCount == 1 ? "page" : "pages"
    println("\(printItem.title!) has \(printItem.pageCount) \(pageString)")
```

```
    if let bookItem = printItem as? Book {
      println(bookItem.tableOfContents)
    }
  } else {
    println("\(item.title) is a video")
  }
}
/*
Prints:
Transitioning to Swift has 200 pages
  Table Of Contents
  ...
How to Perform a Lightweight Core Data Migration has 25 pages
How To Use Xcode Behaviors is a video
*/
```

Summary

Protocols provide a blueprint from which classes, structures, and enumerations can be constructed to specified requirements. Instances can also be checked for conformance to, or temporarily casted as, a protocol type. This chapter compared protocols in Objective-C and Swift, highlighting similarities in usage and differences in syntax, and it introduced the expanded scope of use protocols have in Swift.

Chapter 9

Subclassing and Extending

As stated in the introduction to the previous chapter, Swift is predominantly a protocol-based language. That said, the Swift standard library utilizes extensions expansively to build out the capabilities of its classes, structures, and enumerations. Following suit, this design pattern should also be adopted in custom code. When it comes to expanding the capabilities of a class, however, a choice must be made whether to subclass or extend. Subclassing provides certain capabilities not possible with extensions. In this chapter, the capabilities afforded by subclassing and extending will be explored in Swift, compared to each other and their counterparts in Objective-C.

Subclassing

Subclassing is a core tenet of object-oriented programming. Chapter 7 explained that Swift classes are not reliant on inheriting from a base class. This is not to suggest any less of a commitment to maintaining an object-oriented hierarchy to model abstract and real-world entities in code; and a class that does not inherit from a base class becomes itself a base class that can be subclassed or extended as appropriate. Subclassing provides maximum flexibility to further enable a class or refine (i.e., override) its existing capabilities. In contrast with Objective-C, Swift requires explicit indicators such as the `override` modifier to indicate when overriding a superclass method or property, or the `final` modifier to indicate that a method or property cannot be overridden by a subclass, to provide clarity of intention and prevent undesired overrides. An entire class can be marked `final` to prevent subclassing it altogether. Table 7-2 in Chapter 7 compares the basic syntax for defining classes that inherit from a superclass in Objective-C and Swift.

Initializer Inheritance

Remember from Chapter 7 that all classes must have at least one designated initializer (which may be inherited), and can optionally have one or more convenience initializers (marked with the `convenience` modifier). These initializers call each other or call up through the inheritance chain (also referred to as "delegate to") in a predictable manner following these rules:

1. Convenience initializers can delegate to either another convenience initializer or a designated initializer in the *same class*

2. Designated initializers can only call a designated initializer in the *immediate superclass* (if there is one)

> **Tip** Convenience initializers call `self.init()`. Designated initializers call `super.init()`.

> **Note** A failable initializer can call a nonfailable initializer; however, a nonfailable initializer *cannot* call a failable initializer. If a failable initializer fails, the entire initialization process will fail immediately at the point of the failure and no further initialization code will be executed. See Chapter 7 for coverage of failable initializers.

In Objective-C, a subclass inherits its superclass' initializers. This is not the case in Swift, by default. However, a subclass will automatically inherit its superclass' designated and/or convenience initializers as follows:

1. The subclass must provide default values for any new properties it defines

2. A subclass will automatically inherit all of its superclass' designated initializers if it does not define *any* designated initializers of its own

3. A subclass will automatically inherit all of its superclass' convenience initializers if it either does not define a designated initializer of its own (i.e., #2) or if it overrides *all* of the superclass' designated initialers

All newly introduced nonoptional properties of a subclass must be set during initialization, before calling super, such as accessing properties or calling methods of the superclass in a designated initializer. An initializer can call another initializer to perform a portion of the initialization and avoid writing duplicate code, such as to set some default property values; this process is referred to as *initializer delegation*. A designated initializer of the base class must call a designated initializer of the superclass to give it the opportunity to initialize all its nonoptional properties, and so on, all the way up the inheritance chain. Only once all nonoptional properties in a subclass and its superclass have been set can a method of the subclass or superclass be called. An exception to this otherwise strict sequence—as demonstrated in Table 9-1—is when a property of the subclass requires initialization of the superclass, in which case the superclass initializer is called before initializing the dependent property of the subclass.

Overriding

Marking an initializer with the `required` modifier will mandate that its subclasses override it, unless it is automatically inherited. The `required` modifier must also be used in a subclass' implementation, instead of writing the `override` modifier for a designated initializer. A subclass convenience initializer can override a superclass designated initializer, in which case the initializer definition must be marked with the `override` modifier. A subclass initializer can *match* a superclass convenience initializer; however, because convenience initializers can only call initializers in the same class, a superclass convenience initializer being matched is not callable from within a subclass convenience initializer.

> **Note** A nonfailable initializer can override a failable initializer, but a failable initializer *cannot* override a nonfailable initializer.

A property must be declared as a variable in the superclass in order to allow a subclass to modify it, even during initialization. A stored property can be overridden to add custom accessors or property observers. A read-only (getter only) property can be overridden to make it read-write (i.e., by also implementing a setter). However, a read-write property cannot be overridden to make it read-only. A stored or computed property can be overridden with a computed property. Call the superclass' getter (e.g., `super.propertyName`) when it is not necessary to override the superclass' implementation of the getter.

Overriding methods in Swift follows the same rules as for overriding properties. Write the `override` modifier at the beginning of a method override definition, the `final` modifier to prevent a method from being overridden, and use `super` to call the superclass' version of a method (e.g., `super.functionName()`). The compiler will also provide helpful guidance if, for example, the `override` modifier is inadvertently not written in when it should be.

> **Tip** To implement a method override, just start typing the function name and Xcode will offer code-completion. Once the desired method is selected, press **tab** and Xcode will write in the complete override definition, including `override func` and the method body, as illustrated in Figure 9-1.

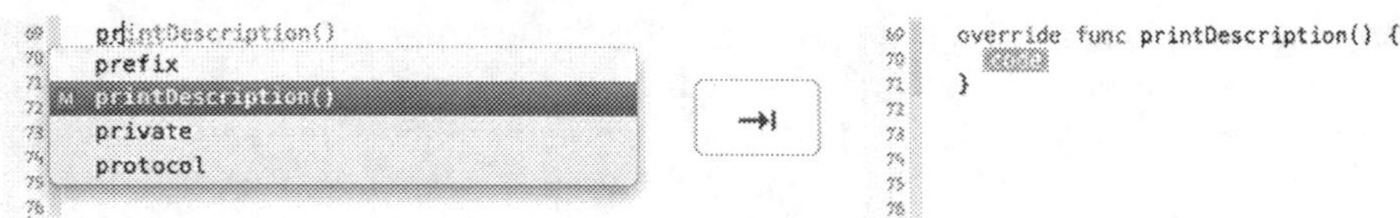

***Figure 9-1.** Code-completion for overridden method in Swift*

Deinitializer Inheritance

A subclass automatically inherits a superclass' deinitializer, and the superclass deinitializer is automatically called after the subclass deinitializer is called, even if the subclass does not implement an explicit deinitializer.

Table 9-1 compares subclassing in Objective-C and Swift. Notice that the same issue with `deinit` not being consistently called in a playground, as mentioned in Chapter 7, also applies here; however, if the code is run in a full Xcode project, the `println()`s in the `deinit` methods will be printed out.

Table 9-1. Comparison of subclassing in Objective-C and Swift

Objective-C	`// In CustomClass.h`
	`@import UIKit;`
	`@interface Value : NSObject`
	`@property (assign, nonatomic) NSInteger integerProperty;`
	`@property (assign, nonatomic) CGFloat doubleProperty;`
	`@property (copy, nonatomic, readonly) NSString *description;`
	`- (instancetype)initWithInteger:(NSInteger)integer`
	`double:(CGFloat)doubleValue string:(NSString *)string;`
	`- (NSString *)stringProperty;`
	`- (void)setStringProperty:(NSString *)string;`
	`- (void)printDescription;`
	`@end`
	`@interface ValueArray : Value`
	`@property (copy, nonatomic) NSArray *integerArray;`
	`@property (copy, nonatomic) NSArray *doubleArray;`
	`@property (copy, nonatomic) NSArray *stringArray;`
	`@property (assign, nonatomic) NSInteger count;`
	`- (instancetype)initWithInteger:(NSInteger)integer`
	`double:(CGFloat)doubleValue string:(NSString *)string`
	`count:(NSInteger)count;`
	`- (instancetype)initWithInteger:(NSInteger)integer`
	`double:(CGFloat)doubleValue string:(NSString *)string;`
	`@end`
	`// In CustomClass.m`
	`#import "CustomClass.h"`
	`@interface Value ()`
	`@property (copy, nonatomic) NSString`
	`*changingCaseStringProperty;`
	`@end`
	`@implementation Value`
	`- (instancetype)initWithInteger:(NSInteger)integer`
	`double:(CGFloat)doubleValue string:(NSString *)string`
	`{`
	`  if (self = [super init]) {`
	`    _integerProperty = integer;`
	`    _doubleProperty = doubleValue;`
	`    _changingCaseStringProperty = string.lowercaseString;`
	`  }`
	`  return self;`
	`}`

(continued)

Table 9-1. (*continued*)

```
- (NSString *)stringProperty
{
  return self.changingCaseStringProperty;
}
- (void)setStringProperty:(NSString *)string
{
  self.changingCaseStringProperty = string.lowercaseString;
}
- (NSString *)description
{
  return [NSString stringWithFormat:@"Values: %li, %.1f, %@",
  (long)self.integerProperty, self.doubleProperty, [self
  stringProperty]];
}
- (void)printDescription
{
  NSLog(@"%@", self.description);
}
- (void)dealloc
{
  NSLog(@"Value deallocated");
}
@end
@implementation ValueArray
- (instancetype)initWithInteger:(NSInteger)integer
double:(CGFloat)doubleValue string:(NSString *)string
count:(NSInteger)count
{
  if (self = [super initWithInteger:integer
  double:doubleValue string:string]) {
    [self setStringProperty:string.uppercaseString];
    NSMutableArray *integerArray = [@[] mutableCopy];
    NSMutableArray *doubleArray = [@[] mutableCopy];
    NSMutableArray *stringArray = [@[] mutableCopy];
```

(*continued*)

Table 9-1. (*continued*)

```
      for (int i = 0; i < count; i++) {
        [integerArray addObject:@(integer)];
        [doubleArray addObject:@(round(doubleValue * 10) / 10)];
        [stringArray addObject:[self stringProperty]];
        _integerArray = integerArray;
        _doubleArray = doubleArray;
        _stringArray = stringArray;
        _count = count;
      }
      [self printDescription];
    }
    return self;
}
- (instancetype)initWithInteger:(NSInteger)integer
double:(CGFloat)doubleValue string:(NSString *)string
{
  return [self initWithInteger:integer double:doubleValue
  string:string count:3];
}
- (NSString *)stringProperty
{
  return self.changingCaseStringProperty;
}
- (void)setStringProperty:(NSString *)string
{
  self.changingCaseStringProperty = string.uppercaseString;
}
- (NSString *)description
{
  return [NSString stringWithFormat:@"Value arrays (%li per
  array):\n%@\n%@\n%@", (long)self.count, self.integerArray,
  self.doubleArray, self.stringArray];
}
- (void)printDescription
{
  NSLog(@"%@", super.description);
  NSLog(@"%@", self.description);
}
```

(*continued*)

Table 9-1. (*continued*)

```
- (void)dealloc
{
  NSLog(@"ValueArray deallocated");
}
@end
// In -[SomeOtherClass someMethod] in SomeOtherClass.m
Value *value = [[Value alloc] initWithInteger:1 double:2.3f
string:@"CHARLIE"];
[value printDescription]; // Prints "Values: 1, 2.3, charlie"
__unused ValueArray *valueArray1 = [[ValueArray alloc]
initWithInteger:1 double:1.2f string:@"delta"];
/* Prints:
Values: 1, 1.2, DELTA
Value arrays:
(1, 1, 1)
("1.2", "1.2", "1.2")
(DELTA, DELTA, DELTA)
*/
__unused ValueArray *valueArray2 = [[ValueArray alloc]
initWithInteger:8 double:7.6f string:@"echo" count:4];
/* Prints:
Values: 8, 7.6, ECHO
Value arrays:
(8, 8, 8, 8)
("7.6", "7.6", "7.6", "7.6")
(ECHO, ECHO, ECHO, ECHO)
*/
valueArray1 = nil;
/* Prints:
ValueArray deallocated
Value deallocated
...
*/
```

(*continued*)

Table 9-1. (*continued*)

Swift	<pre>import Foundation
	class Value {
	  var integerProperty = 0
	  var doubleProperty = 0.0
	  var changingCaseStringProperty = ""
	  var stringProperty: String {
	    get {
	      return changingCaseStringProperty
	    }
	    set {
	      changingCaseStringProperty = newValue.lowercaseString
	    }
	  }
	  var description: String {
	    return "Values: \(integerProperty), \(doubleProperty),
	    \(stringProperty)"
	  }
	  final var valueArray: ValueArray {
	    let valueArray = ValueArray(integer: integerProperty,
	    double: doubleProperty, string: stringProperty)
	    return valueArray
	  }
	  required init(integer: Int, double: Double, string: String) {
	    integerProperty = integer
	    doubleProperty = double
	    stringProperty = string
	  }
	  func printDescription() {
	    println(description)
	  }
	  deinit {
	    println("Value deallocated")
	  }
	}
	class ValueArray: Value {
	  override var stringProperty: String {
	    get {
	      return super.changingCaseStringProperty
	    }
	    set {
	      super.changingCaseStringProperty = newValue.uppercaseString
	    }
	  }</pre>

(*continued*)

Table 9-1. (*continued*)

```
  var integerArray: [Int]!
  var doubleArray: [Double]!
  var stringArray: [String]!
  var count: Int
  override var description: String {
    return "Value arrays (\(count) per array):\n\
    (integerArray)\n\(doubleArray)\n\(stringArray)"
  }
  init(integer: Int, double: Double, string: String,
  count: Int) {
    self.count = count
    integerArray = [Int](count: count, repeatedValue: integer)
    doubleArray = [Double](count: count, repeatedValue: double)
    super.init(integer: integer, double: double, string: string)
    stringArray = [String](count: count, repeatedValue:
    stringProperty)
    printDescription()
  }
  required convenience init(integer: Int, double: Double,
  string: String) {
    self.init(integer: integer, double: double, string:
    string, count: 3)
  }
  override func printDescription() {
    println(super.description)
    println(description)
  }
  deinit {
    println("ValueArray deallocated")
  }
}
let value = Value(integer: 1, double: 2.3, string: "CHARLIE")
value.printDescription() // Prints "Values: 1, 2.3, charlie"
var valueArray1: ValueArray? = value.valueArray
/* Prints:
Values: 1, 2.3, CHARLIE
Value arrays (3 per array):
[1, 1, 1]
[2.3, 2.3, 2.3]
[CHARLIE, CHARLIE, CHARLIE]
*/
```

(*continued*)

Table 9-1. (*continued*)

```
let valueArray2 = ValueArray(integer: 1, double: 2.3, string:
"delta")
/* Prints:
Values: 1, 2.3, DELTA
Value arrays (3 per array):
[1, 1, 1]
[2.3, 2.3, 2.3]
[DELTA, DELTA, DELTA]
*/
let valueArray3 = ValueArray(integer: 8, double: 7.6, string:
"echo", count: 4)
/* Prints:
Values: 8, 7.6, ECHO
Value arrays (4 per array):
[8, 8, 8, 8]
[7.6, 7.6, 7.6, 7.6]
[ECHO, ECHO, ECHO, ECHO]
*/
valueArray1 = nil
/* Prints:
ValueArray deallocated
Value deallocated
...
*/
```

Extending

Extensions in Swift are similar to categories in Objective-C. In Objective-C, they can be used to add methods, including via protocol adoption, to existing classes; however, overriding existing methods is discouraged (behavior is undefined), and categories should not be used to add properties to a class—per Apple documentation, properties will not be synthesized with accessor methods and a value cannot be stored unless it's already stored by the original class. In Swift, extensions allow convenience initializers (but not designated initializers), methods, computed properties (but not stored properties), protocol adoption, and even nested types to be added to existing classes, structures, and enumerations, including types for which the original source code is not available (referred to as *retroactive modeling*). Swift extensions cannot add a deinitializer, nor can they override existing functionality (the compiler will prevent attempts to do so). Regarding classes, this limitation will often be the decisive factor when choosing whether to subclass or extend a class. Unlike categories in Objective-C, Swift extensions are not named. Table 9-2 compares the definition syntax of categories in Objective-C to extensions in Swift.

Table 9-2. ***Definition syntax for Objective-C categories and Swift extensions***

Objective-C	`// In BaseClassName+CategoryName.h`
	`importStatements`
	`@interface BaseClassName (CategoryName) <ProtocolName, ...>`
	`publicMethodDeclarations`
	`@end`
	`// In BaseClassName+CategoryName.m`
	`importStatements`
	`@implementation ClassName (CategoryName) <ProtocolName, ...>`
	`methodImplementations`
	`@end`

Swift	`// In .swift file`
	`extension ClassName: ProtocolName, ... {`
	  `propertyDefinitions`
	  `methodDefinitions`
	`}`

As in Objective-C, in which a block could be used to initialize a property, a Swift closure can also be used in this manner. Similarly, this capability can be implemented in a category or extension. The abstraction of doing so, however, bears a note of caution. If a block or closure is used to initialize a property in a category or extension, remember that the instance has not yet been fully initialized at the point the block/closure is executed, which means that other properties and methods within the block/closure should not be accessed, and `self` should also not be called.

Table 9-3 provides comparative examples of an Objective-C category and Swift extensions. The class examples extend the `Value` classes defined in Table 9-1, and for the Objective-C example, the `Value+PrimeValueArray.h` category header is presumed imported in `SomeOtherClass.m`. (Credit goes to Ash Furrow for the enumeration extension Gist that he published, which puts back a useful feature that was removed during Swift's beta period: `https://github.com/AshFurrow/hasValue/blob/master/hasValue.swift`).

Table 9-3. Comparing an Objective-C category and Swift extensions

<table>
<tr><td>Objective-C class</td><td><pre>
// In Value+PrimeValueArray.h
#import "CustomClass.h"
typedef NSInteger (^RandomPrimeGenerator)();
@interface Value (PrimeValueArray) <NSObject>
@property (assign, nonatomic, readonly) NSInteger
primeIntegerProperty;
@property (strong, nonatomic, readonly) ValueArray
*primeValueArray;
- (BOOL)isEqual:(Value *)value;
@end
// In Value+PrimeValueArray.m
#import "Value+PrimeValueArray.h"
RandomPrimeGenerator randomPrimeGenerator = ^NSInteger{
  start: while (YES) {
    u_int32_t randomInteger = arc4random_uniform(11);
    randomInteger = randomInteger > 1 ? randomInteger : 2;
    for (int i = 2; i <= randomInteger; i++) {
      if (randomInteger != i) {
        if (randomInteger % i == 0) {
          goto start;
        }
      }
    }
    return randomInteger;
  }
};
@implementation Value (PrimeValueArray)
-(NSInteger)primeIntegerProperty
{
  return randomPrimeGenerator();
}
- (ValueArray *)primeValueArray
{
  NSInteger primeInteger = self.primeIntegerProperty;
  NSNumberFormatter *spellOutFormatter = [NSNumberFormatter new];
  spellOutFormatter.numberStyle = kCFNumberFormatterSpellOutStyle;
  NSString *string = [spellOutFormatter stringFromNumber:
  @(primeInteger)];
  ValueArray *valueArray = [[ValueArray alloc] initWithInteger:
  primeInteger double:primeInteger string:string
  count:primeInteger];
  return valueArray;
}
</pre></td></tr>
</table>

(continued)

Table 9-3. (*continued*)

```
- (BOOL)isEqual:(Value *)value
{
  return self.integerProperty == value.integerProperty &&
  self.doubleProperty == value.doubleProperty && [self.
  stringProperty isEqualToString:value.stringProperty];
}
@end
// In -[SomeOtherClass someMethod] in SomeOtherClass.m
Value *value1 = [[Value alloc] initWithInteger:1 double:1.0f
string:@"One"];
__unused ValueArray *valueArray4 = value1.primeValueArray;
/* Prints (for example):
Values: 5, 5, FIVE
Value arrays:
(5, 5, 5, 5, 5)
(5, 5, 5, 5, 5)
(FIVE, FIVE, FIVE, FIVE, FIVE)
*/
Value *value2 = [[Value alloc] initWithInteger:1 double:1.0f
string:@"One"];
while (![value1.primeValueArray isEqual:value2.
primeValueArray]) {
  NSLog(@"No match yet...");
}
/* Prints (for example):
Values: 3, 3, THREE
Value arrays:
(3, 3, 3)
(3, 3, 3)
(THREE, THREE, THREE)
Values: 5, 5, FIVE
Value arrays:
(5, 5, 5, 5, 5)
(5, 5, 5, 5, 5)
(FIVE, FIVE, FIVE, FIVE, FIVE)
No match yet...
Values: 5, 5, FIVE
Value arrays:
(5, 5, 5, 5, 5)
(5, 5, 5, 5, 5)
(FIVE, FIVE, FIVE, FIVE, FIVE)
Values: 5, 5, FIVE
```

(*continued*)

Table 9-3. (*continued*)

	Value arrays: (5, 5, 5, 5, 5) (5, 5, 5, 5, 5) (FIVE, FIVE, FIVE, FIVE, FIVE) */ NSLog(@"We have a match!"); // Prints "We have a match!"

Swift class	let randomPrimeGenerator = {
	  () -> Int in
	  start: while true {
	    var randomInteger = arc4random_uniform(11)
	    randomInteger = randomInteger > 1 ? randomInteger : 2
	    for i in 2...randomInteger {
	      if randomInteger != i {
	        if randomInteger % i == 0 {
	          continue start
	        }
	      }
	    }
	    return Int(randomInteger)
	  }
	}
	func ==(lhs: Value, rhs: Value) -> Bool {
	  return lhs.integerProperty == rhs.integerProperty &&
	  lhs.doubleProperty == rhs.doubleProperty &&
	  lhs.stringProperty == rhs.stringProperty
	}
	extension Value: Equatable {
	  var primeIntegerProperty: Int {
	    return randomPrimeGenerator()
	  }
	  final var primeValueArray: ValueArray {
	    let primeInteger = primeIntegerProperty
	    let spellOutFormatter = NSNumberFormatter()
	    spellOutFormatter.numberStyle = .SpellOutStyle
	    let string = spellOutFormatter.
	    stringFromNumber(primeInteger)!
	    let valueArray = ValueArray(integer: primeInteger,
	    double: Double(primeInteger), string: string, count:
	    primeInteger)
	    return valueArray
	  }
	}

(*continued*)

Table 9-3. (*continued*)

```
let value1 = Value(integer: 1, double: 1.0, string: "One")
let valueArray4 = value1.primeValueArray
/* Prints (for example):
Values: 5, 5.0, FIVE
Value arrays (5 per array):
[5, 5, 5, 5, 5]
[5.0, 5.0, 5.0, 5.0, 5.0]
[FIVE, FIVE, FIVE, FIVE, FIVE]
*/
let value2 = Value(integer: 2, double: 2.0, string: "Two")
while value1.primeValueArray != value2.primeValueArray {
  println("No match yet...")
}
/* Prints (for example):
Values: 3, 3.0, THREE
Value arrays (3 per array):
[3, 3, 3]
[3.0, 3.0, 3.0]
[THREE, THREE, THREE]
Values: 5, 5.0, FIVE
Value arrays (5 per array):
[5, 5, 5, 5, 5]
[5.0, 5.0, 5.0, 5.0, 5.0]
No match yet...
[FIVE, FIVE, FIVE, FIVE, FIVE]
Values: 5, 5.0, FIVE
Value arrays (5 per array):
[5, 5, 5, 5, 5]
[5.0, 5.0, 5.0, 5.0, 5.0]
[FIVE, FIVE, FIVE, FIVE, FIVE]
Values: 5, 5.0, FIVE
Value arrays (5 per array):
[5, 5, 5, 5, 5]
[5.0, 5.0, 5.0, 5.0, 5.0]
[FIVE, FIVE, FIVE, FIVE, FIVE]
*/
println("We have a match!") // Prints "We have a match!"
```

(*continued*)

Table 9-3. (*continued*)

Swift structure	<pre>extension String {
	  var reversedString: String {
	    let reversedValueArray = reverse(self)
	    return "".join(reversedValueArray.map { String($0) })
	  }
	  var isPalindromic: Bool {
	    return self.lowercaseString == reversedString.
	    lowercaseString
	  }
	}
	let string = "AManAPlanACanalPanama"
	println(string.isPalindromic) // Prints "true"</pre>

Swift enumeration	<pre>extension Optional {
	  var hasValue: Bool {
	    switch self {
	    case .None:
	      return false
	    case .Some(_):
	      return true
	    }
	  }
	}
	var optionalString: String?
	println(optionalString.hasValue) // Prints "false"
	optionalString = "Hello world"
	println(optionalString.hasValue) // Prints "true"</pre>

Protocol Adoption Via An Extension

An extension can be used to add protocol adoption and conformance to a type. However, a type that satisfies the requirements of a protocol does *not* implicitly or automatically adopt that protocol. In this case, an empty extension can be used to explicitly declare adoption of the protocol. The following example demonstrates both scenarios:

```
@objc protocol Describable {
  var description: String { get }
}
class ClassOne { }
class ClassTwo {
  var description = "ClassTwo"
}
```

```
class ClassThree {
  var description = "ClassThree"
}
extension ClassOne: Describable {
  var description: String {
    return "ClassOne"
  }
}
extension ClassThree: Describable { }
let arrayOfClasses = [ClassOne(), ClassTwo(), ClassThree()]
for value in arrayOfClasses {
  if value is Describable {
    println(value.description)
  }
}
/* Prints:
ClassOne
ClassThree
*/
```

Summary

Consider the juxtaposition of protocols, extensions, and subclasses in Swift: protocols establish expected behavior and state, whereas extensions directly append desired capabilities (as well as protocol adoption), and subclassing allows for further refining and broadening the capabilities of a class. Together, these mechanisms facilitate writing code that is expressive, easy to follow, decoupled (except when coupling is desired), and extensible. The Swift standard library is brimming with protocols and extensions. Taking a cue from the engineers who created Swift, your code should also embrace these paradigms and take advantage of these features. Subclassing should be used where necessary, such as when it is semantically appropriate to couple another class to a parent class in order to inherit its capabilities yet maintain type uniqueness between the two classes.

Chapter 10

Controlling Access

As alluded to in Chapter 2, Swift takes an innovative and broad-based approach to access control. This is especially evident when compared with Objective-C, where true access control is limited to instance variables—of which usage has been discouraged in favor of properties for several years. This chapter will provide an example of how circumventing intentional access control can be achieved, followed by an in-depth explanation of access control in Swift, aided by examples to help demonstrate each use case.

Access Control Compared

In Objective-C, stored value access control is limited to instance variables declared in `@implementation`, and method access control is truly not possible. Use of categories can help to hide methods that are intended to be private. However, if the name of a method defined only in a class extension or a category's `@implementation` is correctly guessed, `-[NSObject performSelector:]` (or variations) can successfully be used to call the method. This includes accessors to get or set the value of a property declared only in a class extension. And access to an instance variable declared in `@implementation` can still be achieved if there is a private method that accesses that instance variable. The following example demonstrates this:

```
// In CustomClass.h
@import Foundation;
@interface CustomClass : NSObject
- (void)someMethodThatAccessesAPrivateInstanceVariable;
@end
// In CustomClass.m
#import "CustomClass.h"
@interface CustomClass ()
@property (copy, nonatomic) NSString *privatePropertyString;
@end
```

```
@implementation CustomClass
{
  NSString *_privateInstanceVariableString;
}
- (instancetype)init
{
  if (self = [super init]) {
    _privatePropertyString = @"Private property string";
    _privateInstanceVariableString = @"Private instance variable string";
  }
  return self;
}
- (void)printPrivatePropertyString
{
  NSLog(@"%@", self.privatePropertyString);
}
- (void)someMethodThatAccessesAPrivateInstanceVariable
{
  NSLog(@"%@", _privateInstanceVariableString);
}
@end
// In CustomClass+Additions.h
#import "CustomClass.h"
@interface CustomClass (Additions)
@end
// In CustomClass+Additions.m
#import "CustomClass+Additions.h"
@implementation CustomClass (Additions)
- (void)printCategoryPrivateString
{
  NSLog(@"Private string in category");
}
@end
// In -[SomeOtherClass someMethod] in SomeOtherClass.m that only imports
"CustomClass.h"
CustomClass *customClass = [CustomClass new];
[customClass performSelector:@selector(printPrivatePropertyString)];
[customClass performSelector:@selector(setPrivatePropertyString:)
withObject:@"New private property string"];
NSLog(@"%@", [customClass performSelector:@selector(privatePropertyString)]);
[customClass someMethodThatAccessesAPrivateInstanceVariable];
[customClass performSelector:@selector(printCategoryPrivateString)];
/* Prints:
Private property string
New private property string
Private instance variable string
Private string in category
*/
```

In Swift, access is controlled at the source file and module scopes. A source file typically may contain a single type definition, but it also can contain multiple type definitions as well as independent stored values and functions that are global within the file scope. A module is a single unit of code distribution, such as a build target or framework that can be imported into another module via the `import` keyword. There are three levels of access control to which code may be explicitly marked:

- Public—code is available throughout the module in which it is defined, and to any other source file in another module that imports the defining module
- Internal—code is available throughout the module in which it is defined but may *not* be imported into another source file in another module
- Private—code is available only within the source file in which it is defined

Public provides for the highest level of accessibility, typically suitable for use in the public-facing interface (i.e., the application programming interface, or API) of a framework. Internal is the default access control, implicitly assigned to most types unless explicit access control is specified; exceptions will be noted shortly. Private is the most restrictive level of access control, intended for use in hiding internal implementation.

Generally speaking, a piece of code cannot be marked with a higher level of accessibility than code that it interacts with in any way. For example, a property of a type that is marked internal can only be marked itself as internal or private. A function that takes private values as parameters or returns private values can only be marked itself as private.

Assigning Access Levels

The syntax to explicitly assign an access control level is to write the access modifier `public`, `internal`, or `private` before the declaration or definition of the entity—except for accessors, which will be covered in this section. The following rules apply to implicit, automatic, and explicit assignment of access levels.

A tuple's type can be explicitly assigned, and in the case of a tuple defined in an imported module, the tuple itself *must* be explicitly assigned public access in order to be accessible within the importing module; doing so overrides whatever explicit access control has been assigned to its elements. This behavior is similar to the way mutability is inherited (see Chapter 3 for details).

Enumeration cases are implicitly assigned the same access level as the enumeration itself, and cannot be explicitly assigned another access level. Enumeration associated values cannot have an access level that is more restrictive than the enumeration's access level. See Chapter 7 for coverage of enumeration associated values.

A stored value cannot be assigned a higher access level than its type, and a stored value must be explicitly marked private if its underlying type is private.

A function is implicitly assigned an access level equal to its most restrictive parameter or return value access level. A function can be explicitly assigned an access level equal to or more restrictive than its most restrictive parameter or return value access level.

Initializers may be explicitly assigned an access level equal to or more restrictive than the underlying type's access level, except a required initializer must always be of the same access level as the underlying class. The parameters of an initializer cannot be more restrictive than the intitializer itself. A default initializer is automatically assigned the same type as its underlying type's access level, with two exceptions (see Chapter 7 for coverage of default initializers):

1. For a type defined as public, the default initializer will automatically be assigned internal, and in order to enable an importing module to utilize a default initializer with no parameters, a no-parameter initializer must be defined and explicitly assigned public access.

2. The default memberwise initializer for a structure will automatically be private if any of the structure's stored properties are private, and in order to enable an importing module to utilize a public structure's memberwise initializer, that memberwise initializer must be explicitly defined and assigned as public.

Accessors are implicitly assigned the same access level as underlying type's access level, however, an accessor can be assigned a more restrictive level. The syntax for explicitly assigning a more restrictive access level to an accessor is to write the access level immediately followed by the accessor type keyword in parentheses at the beginning of the declaration or definition, such as `private(set) var someProperty` to restrict access to `someProperty`'s setter to the source file in which it is defined.

A subclass cannot be less restrictive than its superclass; however, it can override a property or method of its superclass and make that entity less restrictive than its superclass.

A nested type is implicitly assigned an access level equal to its enclosing type's access level. Apple's Swift language guide currently states an exception, "If you want a nested type within a public type to be publicly available, you must explicitly declare the nested type as public." However, as demonstrated in exercise 15 in the Suggested Exercises section, assigning the `public` modifier to a nesting type without explicitly assigning the `public` modifier to a type nested within that nesting type does not pose an issue. A nested type may be explicitly assigned a more restrictive access level than that of its enclosing type.

A type can adopt and conform to a protocol that is more restrictive than the type's access level; however, the conforming portion of that type's implementation will be restricted to the access level of the protocol. Individual declarations in a procotol inherit the access level of the protocol itself and cannot be explicitly assigned an access level. A protocol that inherits from one or more protocols cannot be less restrictive than any of the protocols from which it inherits.

Any properties or methods added to a type via an extension will by default have the same default access level as members have by default in the original type, or an extension can be explicitly assigned an access level to set a new default for all newly added properties and methods within that extension. Those members can also individually be explicitly assigned an access level, including one that is less restrictive than the extension itself.

Type aliases are treated as independent types with regards to access control, and can be assigned an access level equal to or more restrictive than the underlying type being aliased.

All other value types, reference types, protocols, and extensions may be explicitly assigned an access level, or will otherwise be implicitly assigned an access level of internal by default.

Table 10-1 provides examples of access control scenarios presented in the preceding text. In order to follow along with these examples, it is necessary to create an Xcode project with two build targets. To do so, launch Xcode from your /Applications folder and select **File ➤ New ➤ Project...** from the menu. In the window that opens select **Application** under the **iOS** section in the left sidebar, select the **Single View Application** template, and click **Next**, as shown in Figure 10-1.

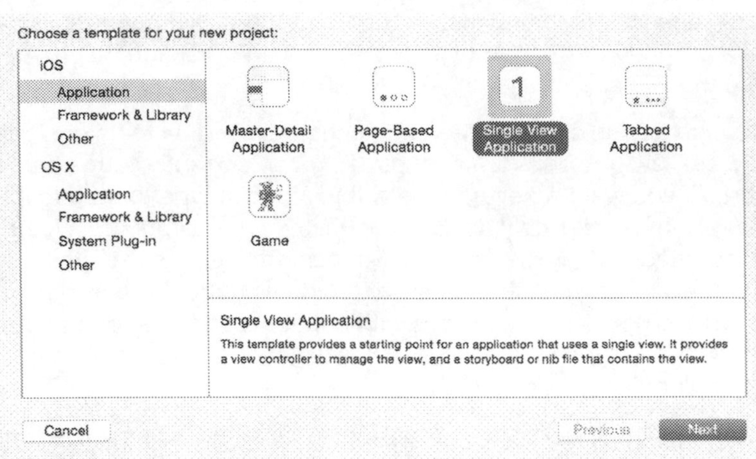

Figure 10-1. Choose a template for your new project

Enter **Transitioning** for the product name, enter an organization name and identifier, select **Swift** for the language, **iPhone** for the device, leave **Use Core Data** unchecked, and click **Next**; Figure 10-2 shows example inputs.

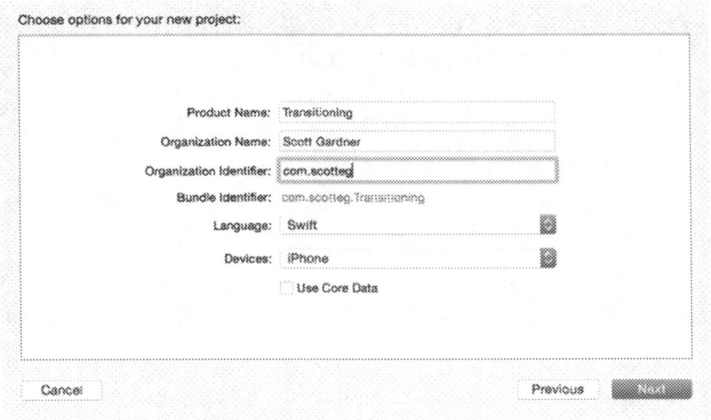

Figure 10-2. Choose options for your new project

Leave **Create Git repository on** unchecked, select a convenient location such as your ~/Documents folder, and click **Create** to save the project, as shown in Figure 10-3.

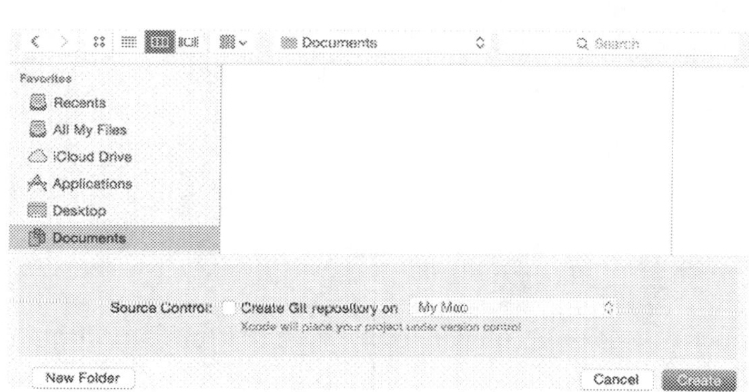

Figure 10-3. Save new Xcode project

Every new Xcode project is created with a main and test target, for example, Transitioning and TransitioningTests, as shown in Figure 10-4.

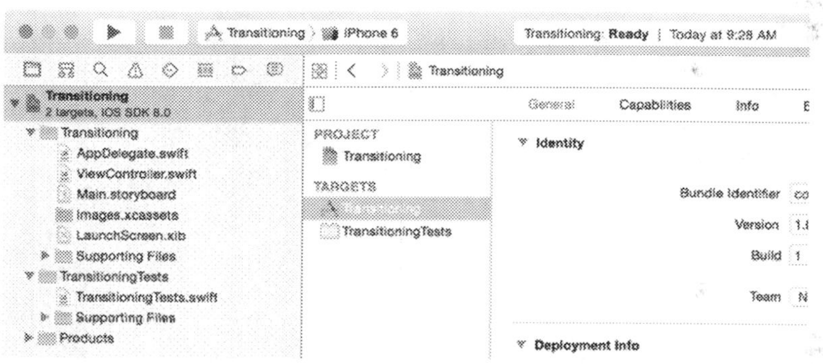

Figure 10-4. Initial Xcode project

The TransitioningTests target is intended for use with unit testing, and although unit testing is a highly encouraged practice, its coverage is beyond the scope of this book. So we will create an additional target in order to demonstrate access control across separate modules. In this case, we'll create a simple framework. Select **File ➤ New ➤ Target...**, and in the dropdown sheet that appears, select **Cocoa Touch Framework** from the **iOS Framework & Library** template list items, and click **Next**, as shown in Figure 10-5.

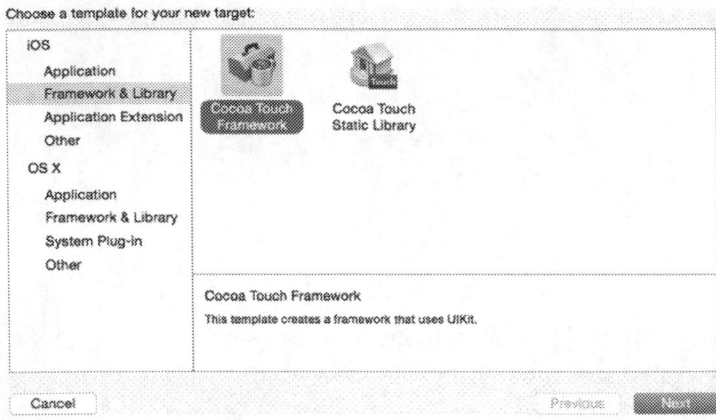

***Figure 10-5.** Choose a template for your new target*

Enter **CustomFramework** for the product name. The other input values should be prefilled with the values entered when the project was created, and click **Finish**. Figure 10-6 demonstrates this.

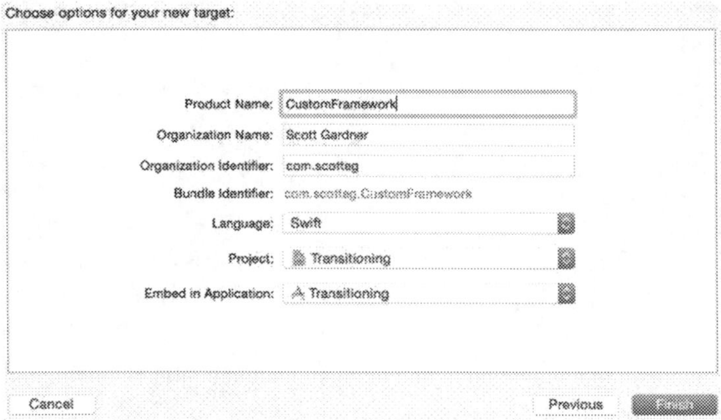

***Figure 10-6.** Choose options for your new target*

Figure 10-7 shows the Xcode project with the newly added target. The circled group folders will be referenced in the following steps.

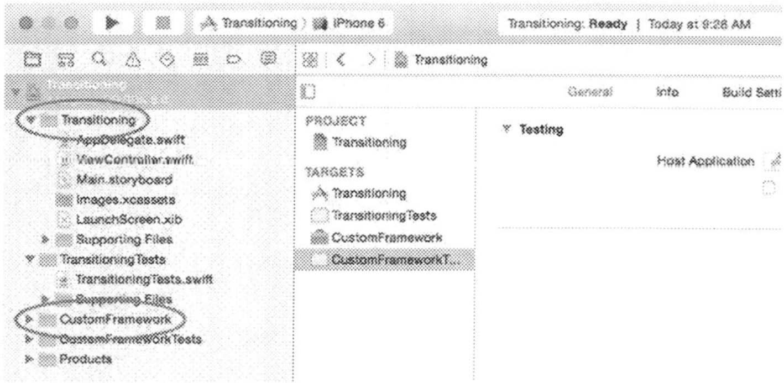

***Figure 10-7.** Xcode project with added target*

Next, we'll add sample Swift source files to the Transitioning and CustomFramework targets. Select the yellow **Transitioning** group folder and select **File ➤ New ➤ File...** from the menu. In the dropdown sheet that appears, select **Swift File** from the **iOS Source** template list items and click **Next**.

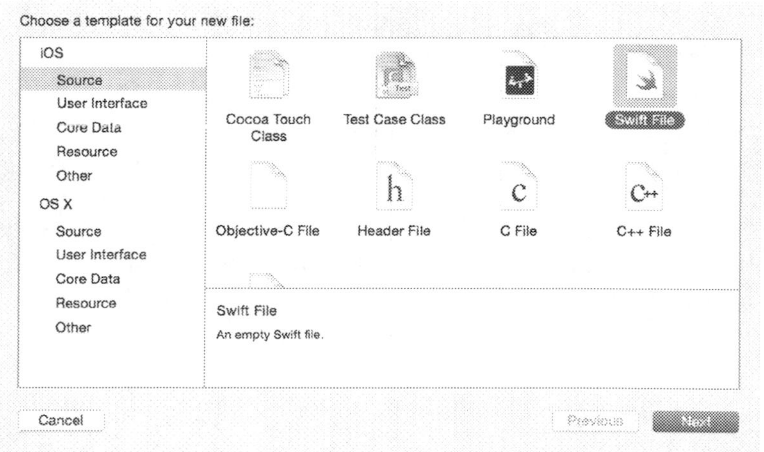

***Figure 10-8.** Choose a template for your new file*

Enter **CustomTypes** for the filename, ensure that the **Transitioning** group and target are selected and checked, respectively, and click **Create**.

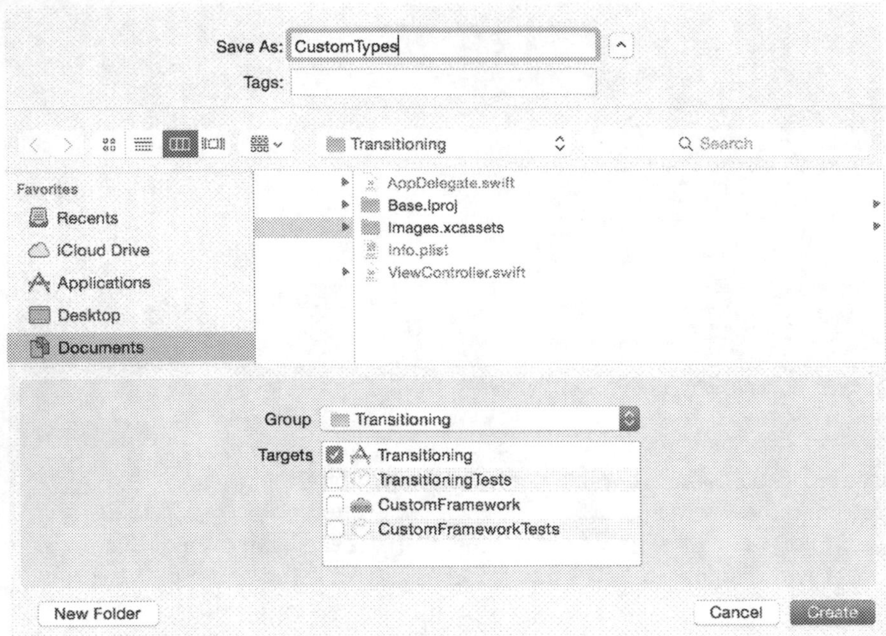

Figure 10-9. Xcode new file Save As

Repeat the last two steps as demonstrated in Figures 10-8 and 10-9, this time selecting the **CustomFramework** group folder in the Project Navigator (circled in Figure 10-7), select **File ➤ New ➤ File...** from the menu, select **Swift File** from the **iOS Source** template list items, click **Next**, name the file **CustomFrameworkTypes**, ensure that the **CustomFramework** group and target are selected and checked, respectively, and click **Create**. Figure 10-10 shows the Xcode project with these new files added.

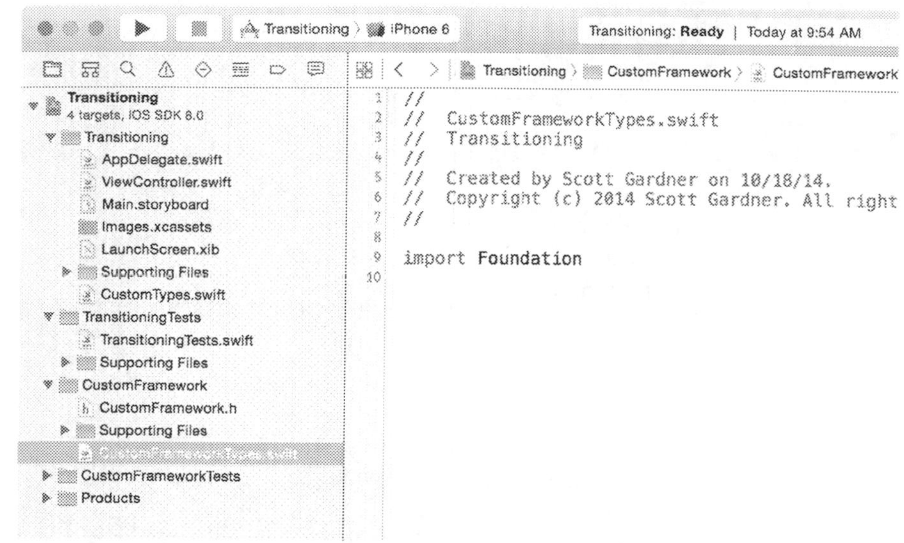

Figure 10-10. Xcode project with added files

With these preparations in place, Table 10-1 provides setup code and examples of each of the aforementioned access control scenarios. All example code is presumed to be entered within the `viewDidLoad()` method (after the setup code) in `ViewController.swift`, unless otherwise noted. Access control has been assigned to each entity to allow access in the example code, and the project will compile. Suggested exercises will be provided after Table 10-1.

Table 10-1. Examples of access control scenarios in Swift

```
// In CustomTypes.swift
import Foundation
private let value1 = 1
private let value2 = "Two"
class CustomClass {
  let tuple = (value1, value2)
}
struct CustomStruct {
  let title = "CustomStruct"
  private(set) var subtitle = ""
}
let customStruct = CustomStruct()
struct Person {
  var name: String
}
```

(continued)

Table 10-1. (*continued*)

```
func printGreeting(greeting: String, #to: Person) {
  println("\(greeting) \(to.name)!")
}
class City {
  let name: String!
  required init(name: String) {
    self.name = name
    println(name)
  }
}
struct AnotherStruct {
  let customStruct: CustomStruct
  init() {
    customStruct = CustomStruct()
    customStruct.subtitle = "A New Subtitle"
    println(customStruct.subtitle) // Prints "A New Subtitle"
  }
}
class PrivateTitleClass {
  private var title: String {
    return "PrivateTitleClass"
  }
}
class AccessibleTitleSubclass: PrivateTitleClass {
  override var title: String {
    return super.title
  }
}
struct NestingStruct {
  let nestedStruct = NestedStruct()
  struct NestedStruct {
    var title = "NestedStruct"
    init() {
      println(title)
    }
  }
}
protocol HasTitle {
  var title: String { get set }
}
```

(*continued*)

Table 10-1. (*continued*)

```
protocol HasSubtitle: HasTitle {
  var subtitle: String { get set }
}
extension CustomClass {
  var title: String {
    return "CustomClass"
  }
  var subtitle: String {
    return "A Catchy Subtitle"
  }
}
// In CustomFrameworkTypes.swift
import Foundation
private let value1 = 1
private let value2 = "Two"
public class CustomFrameworkClass {
  public var tuple = (value1, value2)
    public init() { }
}
public struct CustomFrameworkStruct {
  public let title = "CustomFrameworkStruct"
  public init() { }
}
public enum CustomFrameworkEnum {
  case One
  case TwoWithAssociatedValue(CustomFrameworkStruct)
}
public typealias CFStruct = CustomFrameworkStruct
// In ViewController.swift
import UIKit
import CustomFramework
class ViewController: UIViewController {
  override func viewDidLoad() {
    super.viewDidLoad()
    // Enter forthcoming example code here
  }
}
```

(*continued*)

Table 10-1. (*continued*)

Tuple	`let customClass = CustomClass()`
	`let customFrameworkClass = CustomFrameworkClass()`
	`println(customClass.tuple) // Prints "(1, Two)"`
	`println(customFrameworkClass.tuple) // Prints "(1, Two)"`
	`customFrameworkClass.tuple.0 = 3`
	`customFrameworkClass.tuple.1 = "Four"`
	`println(customFrameworkClass.tuple) // Prints "(3, Four)"`

Enumeration	`let customFrameworkEnum = CustomFrameworkEnum.`
	`TwoWithAssociatedValue(CustomFrameworkStruct())`
	`switch customFrameworkEnum {`
	`  case .One:`
	`    println("One")`
	`    case .TwoWithAssociatedValue(let customFrameworkStruct):`
	`    println(customFrameworkStruct.title)`
	`}`
	`// Prints "CustomFrameworkStruct"`

Stored value	`let customStruct = CustomStruct()` `println(customStruct.title) // Prints "CustomStruct"`
Function	`printGreeting("Hello", to: Person(name: "Charlotte"))` `// Prints "Hello Charlotte!"`
Initializer	`let boston = City(name: "Boston") // Prints "Boston"`
Accessor	`let anotherStruct = AnotherStruct() // Prints "A New` `Subtitle"`

Subclass override	`var accessibleTitleSubclass = AccessibleTitleSubclass()`
	`println(accessibleTitleSubclass.title) // Prints`
	`"PrivateTitleClass"`

Nested type	`let nestingStruct = NestingStruct() // Prints "NestedStruct"`
	`println(nestingStruct.nestedStruct.title) // Prints`
	`"NestedStruct"`

Protocol	`struct Media: HasSubtitle {`
	`  var title = "A Good Title"`
	`  var subtitle = "A Catchy Subtitle"`
	`}`
	`let media = Media()`
	`println(media.subtitle) // Prints "A Catchy Subtitle"`

Extension	`println(customClass.title) // Prints "CustomClass"`
Type alias	`let cfStruct = CFStruct()` `println(cfStruct.title) // Prints "CustomFrameworkStruct"`

SUGGESTED EXERCISES

The following exercises will demonstrate each of the rules mentioned in the Assigning Access Levels section. For each of the exercises listed here, select **Product ➤ Run** from the menu to observe specified output, and be sure to undo changes after each exercise in order to restore the project to a compilable status and expected state for the next exercise. A build (**Product ➤ Build** from the menu, or **command** + **B**) may be necessary to clear remnant compiler errors:

1. Add the `private` modifier to the `CustomClass` definition in CustomTypes.swift. Observe the compiler warning: Use of unresolved identifier 'CustomClass'

2. Comment out `import CustomFramework` in ViewController.swift. Observe the multiple compiler errors including: Use of unresolved identifier 'CustomFrameworkClass'

3. Comment out the empty initializer in `CustomFrameworkClass` in CustomFrameworkTypes.swift. Observe the compiler error: 'CustomFrameworkClass' cannot be constructed because it has no accessible initializers

4. Delete the `public` modifier from the `tuple` variable definition in `CustomFrameworkClass` in CustomFrameworkTypes.swift. Observe observe the multiple compiler errors: 'CustomFrameworkClass' does not have a member named 'tuple'

5. Change the access level modifier of the `CustomFrameworkStruct` definition in CustomFrameworkTypes.swift to `private`. Observe the compiler error: Enum case in a public enum uses a private type

6. Delete the `public` modifier from the `title` variable definition in `CustomFrameworkStruct` in CustomFrameworkTypes.swift. Observe the compiler error: 'CustomFrameworkStruct' does not have a member named 'title'

7. Add the `public` modifier to the `title` constant definition in `CustomStruct` in CustomTypes.swift. Observe the compiler warning: Declaring a public let for an internal struct

8. In CustomTypes.swift, add the `private` modifier to the `CustomStruct` definition. Observe the compiler error on the `customStruct` constant in CustomTypes.swift: Constant must be declared private because its type 'CustomStruct' uses a private type

9. Add the `private` modifier to the `Person` definition in CustomTypes.swift. Observe the compiler error on the `printGreeting(_:to:)` function: Function must be declared private because its parameter uses a private type

10. Add a `public` modifier to the `required init(name:)` definition in `City` in CustomTypes.swift. Observe the compiler warning: Declaring a public initializer for an internal class

11. Delete the `public` modifier from the `init()` method definition in `CustomFrameworkStruct` in CustomFrameworkTypes.swift. Observe the compiler error: 'CustomFrameworkStruct' cannot be constructed because it has no accessible initializers

12. Add the `private` modifier to the `name` variable definition in `Person` in CustomTypes.swift. Observe the compiler error: 'Person' cannot be constructed because it has no accessible initializers

13. Add the following line of code at the end of the `viewDidLoad()` method in ViewController.swift and observe the compiler error: Cannot assign to 'subtitle' in 'customStruct':

    ```
    customStruct.subtitle = "A new subtitle"
    ```

14. Add the `public` modifier to the `AccessibleTitleSubclass` definition in CustomTypes.swift. Observe the compiler error: Class cannot be declared public because its superclass is internal

15. Add the `public` modifier to the `NestingStruct` definition in CustomTypes.swift. Observe that no compliler error is thrown

16. Add the `public` modifier to the `NestedStruct` definition in `NestingStruct` in CustomTypes.swift. Observe the compiler warning: declaring a public struct for an internal struct

17. Add the `private` modifier to the `nestedStruct` constant in `NestingStruct` in CustomTypes.swift. Observe the compilier error on the `println()` function in ViewController.swift: 'NestingStruct' does not have a member named 'nestedStruct'

18. Add the `private` modifier to the `HasSubtitle` definition in CustomTypes.swift and observe the compiler error on the `Media` definition in ViewController.swift: Use of undeclared type 'HasSubtitle'

19. Add the `public` modifier to the `HasSubtitle` definition in CustomTypes.swift and observe the compiler error: Public protocol cannot refine an internal protocol

20. Add the `private` modifier to the `subtitle` definition in `HasSubtitle` in CustomTypes.swift and observe the compiler error: 'private' modifier cannot be used in protocols

21. Add the `private` modifier to the `CustomClass extension` definition in CustomTypes.swift and observe the compiler errors in ViewController.swift: 'CustomClass' does not have a member named 'title'; and, 'CustomClass' does not have a member named 'subtitle'

22. In CustomTypes.swift, add the `private` modifier to the `CustomClass extension` definition, add the `public` modifier to the `title` definition within that extension, and add the `internal` modifier to the `subtitle` definition within that extension. Observe the compiler warnings on the `title` and `subtitle` definition, respectively: Declaring a public var in a private extension; and, Delcaring an internal var in a private extension. Yet also notice that there are no compiler errors on the `println(customClass.title)` and `println(customClass.subtitle)` code in ViewController.swift

23. Delete the `public` modifier from the `CFStruct` definition in CustomFrameworkTypes.swift and observe the compiler error in ViewController.swift: Use of unresolved identifier 'CFStruct'

These exercises explore a wide variety of access control scenarios that you may need to implement or will encounter in Swift. It would be worthwhile to go beyond these exercises and try changing, removing, or adding access control assignments to this or any other Swift code, and observe the results.

Summary

Access control in Swift enables managing the scope of nearly every type in Swift, while simultaneously alleviating the burdon of explicitly importing types throughout a project or cluttering up a prefix header file—in which one must also be concerned with order of imports. The rules of engagement for assigning access levels are as explicit as the control that they facilitate, and coming from Objective-C, access control in Swift may take some getting used to at first. However, with a dedicated effort to understanding and embracing these new capabilities, access control in Swift can prevent a multitude of issues resulting from the lack of it in Objective-C by ensuring that your code is consumed precisely as intended.

Chapter 11

Generic Programming

Up to this point in this book, function and method parameter and return value types have been explicitly specified. Overloading offers a way to define multiple functions that share the same signature except for varying parameter and/or return value types. And protocols provide for declaring a set of requirements that an adopting type must contractually fulfill. Yet there is one more feature of Swift that may at first feel like a mere combination of aforementioned capabilities; however, in due time, it may prove to be one the most powerful features of the language: generics. As much as the Swift standard library is made up of protocols and extensions, generic types are more abundantly used than the other two combined. Objective-C does not facilitate true generic programming. As such, this chapter will focus on introducing and explaining how to use Swift generics to write more powerful, flexible, and reusable code, without sacrificing type safety.

Specific versus Generic

Stored value types are either implicitly inferred or explicitly stated. Function parameter and return value types have, to this point, also been type-specific. And although the use of `Any` or `AnyObject` (or its type alias, `AnyClass`) can provide a way of being nonspecific about type, working with such values can quickly lead to code that is littered with type checking and casting, and type safety is generally lost. Generics, by contrast, offer a clean way to write code that defers type specification until instantiation or use—that is often more succinct than comparative nongeneric code—and additional requirements may optionally be defined that a generic type must abide by. What's more, generics preserve type safety, one of the hallmarks of Swift.

Forms of generic syntax were briefly demonstrated in Chapter 2 with the example `Optional<String>`, and in Chapter 3, wherein an array and dictionary were defined using the syntax `Array<Type>` and `Dictionary<KeyType, ValueType>`, respectively. In fact, Swift `Array` and `Dictionary` types are actually generic collections in which the value type that an array can hold, or the key and value types that a dictionary can hold, are specified in angle brackets immediately following the collection type name:

```
var intArray: Array<Int> // An array of type Int
var intStringDictionary: Dictionary<Int, String> // A dictionary that can
hold key-value pairs of type Int and String, respectively
```

The types are explicitly specified in the previous example, yet the types could also have been specified using a protocol, for example, expressing that any type that conforms to that protocol can be added as a value to the collection:

```
class CustomClass: Printable {
  var description = "CustomClass"
}
struct CustomStruct: Printable {
  var description = "CustomClass"
}
enum CustomEnum: String, Printable {
  case One = "One"
  case Two = "Two"
  var description: String {
    return "CustomEnum.\(self.rawValue)"
  }
}
let customClass = CustomClass()
let customStruct = CustomStruct()
let customEnum = CustomEnum.One
var arrayOfPrintableItems: Array<Printable> = [customClass, customStruct,
customEnum]
var dictionaryOfPrintableItems: Dictionary<Int, Printable> = [1:
customClass, 2: customStruct, 3: customEnum]
```

Syntax

Going beyond the precursor examples in the last section, custom functions (including initializers and methods), types (including classes, structures, and enumerations), and protocols can be defined using generics, optionally with additional requirements placed on the generic types.

Functions and Types

The syntax for defining functions and types using generics is to enclose a *generic parameter list* in angle brackets immediately after the name. A generic parameter list is made up of one or more *type parameters* that each act as an abstract placeholder, each also optionally paired with a *constraint*. A placeholder is simply a name, typically T to represent the first generic type, U to represent the second generic type, and so on, but any valid type name can be used.

> **Note** A generic type parameter name must follow the same rules as type names in general (see the Naming section in Chapter 2 for details). That said, Apple suggests using a single uppercase letter character, except in cases in which longer, more descriptive names are necessary.

Once defined, a generic type parameter can be used throughout the definition of the function or type, and all references to a generic type parameter anywhere in the definition will be of the same type represented by the generic type parameter when the function is called or type is instantiated.

A constraint can be used to indicate that the generic type inherits from a specified superclass or adopts a protocol or protocol composition, using the same syntax as defining regular class inheritance or protocol adoption. Table 11-1 provides basic syntax for defining generic functions and types.

Table 11-1. ***Basic syntax for defining generic functions and types in Swift***

Function of type T that takes a parameter of type T	`func functionName<T>(paramOneName: T) {`
	`    statements`
	`}`

Function of a type T that subclasses SomeClass and takes a parameter of type T	`func functionName<T: SomeClass>(paramOneName: T) {`
	`    statements`
	`}`

Function of a type T that adopts ProtocolName and takes a parameter of type T	`func functionName<T: ProtocolName>(paramOneName: T) {`
	`    statements`
	`}`

(continued)

Table 11-1. (*continued*)

Function of types T and U that takes parameters of types T and U and returns a value of type T	func *functionName*<*T*, *U*>(*paramOneName*: *T*, *paramTwoName*: *U*) -> *T* {
	    statements
	    return *valueOfTypeT*
	}

Class of a type T that subclasses ParentClass, with an array property of type T	class *ClassName*<*T*: *ParentClass*> {
	    var *propertyName*: [*T*]!
	}

Structure of a type T that adopts ProtocolName with a property of type T	struct *StructName*<*T*: *ProtocolName*> {
	    var *propertyName*: *T*
	}

Enumeration of type T that has an associated value of type T	enum *EnumName*<*T*> {
	    case *None*
	    case *Some*(*T*)
	}

Where Clauses and Protocol Associated Types

In addition to specifying class inheritance or protocol adoption constraints, a generic parameter list can also contain *where clauses* that further constrain one or more generic type parameters. A where clause is defined by writing the `where` keyword after the generic parameter list, followed by one or more boolean equality checkes.

Protocols can also define generic *associated types* using `typealias` definitions within the protocol definition. The actual types represented by the type aliases are determined when the protocol is adopted, yet the type adopting the protocol can also utilize generics in conforming to the protocol, which has the effect of further deferring determination of the actual types until instantiation or use.

Table 11-2 provides basic syntax for defining constraints using where clauses, defining protocols with generic associated types, and combining the use of where clauses with protocol generic associated types.

Table 11-2. Basic syntax for defining generic constraints using where clauses and defining protocols with generic associated types in Swift

Function with where clause contraining the generic type T to be of a type that adopts Equatable, with two parameters each of type T	`func functionName<T where T: Equatable> (paramOne: T, paramTwo: T) { statements }`
Protocol with generic associated type V and property of type V	`protocol ProtocolOne { typealias V var propertyName: V { get set } }`
Function of types T and U, each conforming to ProtocolOne, with where clause constraining type V of T and type V of U to be the same type	`func functionName<T: ProtocolOne, U: ProtocolOne where T.V == U.V> (paramOne: T, paramTwo: U) { statements }`

Usage Examples

The following example demonstrates a class `Holder` of a generic type T is defined with an `items` array property of type `T`. `Holder` also defines a `subscript` to provide a convenient way to print out the type name that is determined at point of instantiation of a `Holder` instance, along with the value at the specified index. `Holder` can be instantiated with any type and hold that type in its `items` array property, as demonstrated with instances of `Holder` created using both value and reference types:

```
class CustomClass: DebugPrintable {
  var debugDescription = "CustomClass"
}
class Holder<T> {
  var items: [T]
  init(_ items: [T]) {
    self.items = items
  }
  subscript(index: Int) -> String {
    let typeName = _stdlib_getDemangledTypeName(items[index])
    return "\(typeName): \(items[index])"
  }
}
```

```
let intHolder = Holder([1, 2, 3])
println(intHolder.items) // Prints "[1, 2, 3]"
println(intHolder[0]) // Prints "Swift.Int: 1"
let doubleHolder = Holder([1.1, 2.2, 3.3])
println(doubleHolder.items) // Prints "[1.1, 2.2, 3.3]"
println(doubleHolder[0]) // Prints "Swift.Double: 1.1"
let stringHolder = Holder(["One", "Two", "Three"])
println(stringHolder.items) // Prints "[One, Two, Three]"
println(stringHolder[0]) // Prints "Swift.String: One"
let customClassHolder = Holder([CustomClass(), CustomClass(),
CustomClass()])
println(customClassHolder.items) // Prints "[CustomClass, CustomClass,
CustomClass]"
println(customClassHolder.items[0]) // Prints "CustomClass"
```

> **Note** The `DebugPrintable` protocol can be adopted by types that want to customize their textual representation for debugging purposes. The protocol requires implementing the read-only variable `debugDescription`. This is similar to overriding `-[NSObject description]` in Objective-C. At the time of this writing, Swift playgrounds do not properly print out the value of `debugDescription`; however, the value is correctly printed out if run in an Xcode project.

This next example demonstrates use of generics with additional constraints imposed on them. Specifically, a `TrailMix` structure is defined of a type `T` that adopts the `Edible` protocol, where that type `T` also adopts the `Printable` protocol, and `TrailMix` itself also adopts the `Printable` protocol:

```
protocol Edible {
  var name: String { get }
  var caloriesPerServing: Int { get }
}
struct Ingredient: Edible, Printable {
  let name: String
  let caloriesPerServing: Int
  var description: String {
    return "\(name) (\(caloriesPerServing) calories per serving)"
  }
  init(_ name: String, _ caloriesPerServing: Int) {
    self.name = name
    self.caloriesPerServing = caloriesPerServing
  }
}
```

```
struct TrailMix<T: Edible where T: Printable>: Printable {
  var ingredients: [T]
  var description: String {
    var caloriesPerServing = 0
    var description = ""
      let count = countElements(ingredients)
      for ingredient in ingredients {
        caloriesPerServing += ingredient.caloriesPerServing / count
        description += "◦ \(ingredient.description)\n"
      }
      return "Trail mix, calories per serving: \(caloriesPerServing)\
nIngredients:\n\(description)"
  }
  init(_ ingredients: [T]) {
    self.ingredients = ingredients
  }
}
let chocolateChips = Ingredient("Chocolate chips", 201)
let driedFruit = Ingredient("Dried fruit", 85)
let granola = Ingredient("Granola", 113)
let mixedNuts = Ingredient("Mixed nuts", 219)
let miniPretzels = Ingredient("Mini pretzels", 110)
var trailMix = TrailMix([chocolateChips, driedFruit, granola, mixedNuts,
miniPretzels])
println(trailMix.description)
/* Prints:
Trail mix, calories per serving: 144
Ingredients:
◦ Chocolate chips (201 calories per serving)
◦ Dried fruit (85 calories per serving)
◦ Granola (113 calories per serving)
◦ Mixed nuts (219 calories per serving)
◦ Mini pretzels (110 calories per serving)
*/
```

As an example of using generics with enumerations, the following example reimplements the `Optional` enumeration type from the Swift standard library:

```
enum OptionalType<T> {
  case None
  case Some(T)
  init() {
    self = .None
  }
}
var someOptionalValue = OptionalType<String>()
switch someOptionalValue {
case .None:
```

```
  println("No value")
case .Some(let value):
  println(value)
}
// Prints "No value"
someOptionalValue = .Some("Hello world!")
switch someOptionalValue {
case .None:
  println("No value")
case .Some(let value):
  println(value)
}
// Prints "Hello world!"
```

For a final example, a protocol `HasMiddleValue` is defined with a generic associated type T, requiring implementation of a `middle()` method that returns an array of type T. The `Array` type is then extended to adopt `HasMiddleValue` by implementing `middle()` to return an array containing the middle one or two items of an array of type T, based on whether the count of the array is odd or even, respectively:

```
protocol HasMiddleValue {
  typealias T
  func middle() -> [T]?
}
extension Array: HasMiddleValue {
  func middle() -> [T]? {
    if self.count > 0 {
      var middleIndex = self.count / 2 - 1
      var middleArray = [T]()
      if self.count % 2 == 0 {
        let middleIndex1 = middleIndex
        let middleIndex2 = middleIndex1 + 1
        middleArray = [self[middleIndex1], self[middleIndex2]]
      } else {
        middleArray = [self[middleIndex + 1]]
      }
      return middleArray
    }
    return nil
  }
}
let arrayOfEvenNumberOfInts = [1, 2, 3, 4, 5]
println(arrayOfEvenNumberOfInts.middle()!) // Prints "[3]"
let arrayOfOddNumberOfStrings = ["A", "B", "C", "D"]
println(arrayOfOddNumberOfStrings.middle()!) // Prints "[B, C]"
```

Summary

This chapter introduced generic programming in Swift and provided examples of using generics with functions, types, and protocols.

I personally thank you for reading this book, and am honored by this opportunity to help you get started programming in Swift. Please share feedback or ask questions via Twitter (`@scotteg`). Good luck!

Index

A

B

C

D

E

F

G

H

I, J, K

L

M

N

O

P, Q

R

S

T

U

V, W

X, Y, Z